ASCENSION:

BEGINNER'S MANUAL

AN OFFERING

FROM

A FELLOW TRAVELER

Theodore A. Baroody, Jr.

Eclectic Press
Waynesville, North Carolina 28786

Copyright © 1989

by
Theodore A. Baroody, Jr., M.A., D.C.

Illustrations by Janice R. Swanger.

ISBN: 0-9619595-1-7

For information and ordering, contact publisher:

ECLECTIC PRESS
205 Pigeon Street
Waynesville, NC 28786

First Printing 1989.

DEDICATION

To all who would be their own master,

follow their own path,

transmute their body to

LIGHT

through the Law of

- LOVE -

and fulfill the evolutionary destiny —

ASCENSION.

CONTENTS

FOREWORD

ASCENSION is our evolutionary destiny. This means to transmute every cell of the body to total Light and move with complete freedom into any realm we wish. For the attainment of ASCENSION is to embrace all life, integrating every molecule of ourselves. It is the apex of the One Great Law of God — LOVE.

ASCENSION opens us to every transcendent possibility that has been or will be conceived. It is not the route of someone disgruntled with life who wishes to escape, for to express total LOVE is not an escapist mechanism.

Instead, ASCENSION is total involvement in life — here and now. It is the complete, enfolding acceptance of ourselves at every level of BEing where only the purest Light can enter; the Transmutative and ASCENSION process allows nothing less. No devils or mischief-makers can succeed at it. Only the highest and best part of us responds until all parts of the body are living a life of the highest and best.

Along the path of the one who seeks understanding of true spiritual center points are many distracting terms and methodologies. There are -isms, -ists, and -ologies galore. The usual concept of metaphysics is a confusing consideration which lacks not only clarity of total purpose, but the essential vigor of enthusiasm that is necessary to feel our divinely ordered evolutionary destiny.

The thrust of this book is not just to add another "ism," but to incorporate all those which have been found to be valid, into a centralized, coherent focus and to allow the one seeking spiritual balance to bring his own accrued wisdom into an organized, single-eyed approach.

I have written this as a prayer conceived to praise God, the Creator, and as a hymn to celebrate the full resonant feeling of LOVE.

Part I

THE ONE GREAT LAW

Who sees the vision coming?
Who can tell what moment
out of time will be the
seed to root itself,
as swift as lightning
roots into a cloud,
and grow, swifter than
thought, and flower
gigantic in the infinite?

Walk softly through your
forest, and be ready
to hear the horn of horns.

Or in your garden stoop,
but upon your back be ever
conscious of sunlight and
a shadow that may grow.

by Conrad Aiken, 1929

Chapter 1

A NEW VISION

We stand as an oak in late October counting our shattered hopes like so many crinkled leaves and broken limbs in the autumn wind.

We wander through the breezes, searching the heart for an answer to who we are . . . to what we might be.

We feel shut out from any taste of grace, as if God doesn't care or understand, and, of course, never hears. The chest is heavy as we clench our fist against the stars and blast, "Why am I here? What is my purpose? Must I slave in this way for monies just to see the dawn of another day come and pass?"

But a new vision is given. A new hope showers upon us. We can shake in the wet joy of a new BEingness — a new purpose. I bite my tongue as would an excited child with vibrant enthusiasm to share with you this long imbued but little understood, universal knowledge.

We *can* ASCEND. We can actually change the physical body completely into light and ASCEND! This experience is not reserved just for world avatars or regional gurus. God opens the door for all and eagerly awaits.

What stands in the way to ASCENDING? Only lack of total LOVE for God and Self. For the LOVE of God is all-encompassing.

We may be tempted to think that because our past

has been less than noble there is no hope for ASCEN-SION. We may even think that those professing a religion or outwardly living a socially acceptable religious life have the jump on us. This is not so. The dice fall in only two directions. We choose either Life or Death — ASCENSION or the grave.

Death is not inevitable. Just because Methuselah lived 962 years and died doesn't mean we have to. Remember his father, Enoch? He didn't die. He AS-CENDED. He learned completely the One Great Law of LOVE and God took him.

Death of the body is an unnecessary occurrence. We don't have to believe what we've always been told: Everybody dies. We aren't right to believe this archaic thought any more than our ancestors were right to believe that the world was flat. Imagine what a shift in their thinking occurred when Columbus proved to them that it was round.

"But I just clean toilets," or, "I just work in a factory all night," or, "I just clerk in a small store for someone else. How could I ever ASCEND as you say?"

I have heard statements such as these. Only a stubborn desire *not* to go all the way into ASCENSION keeps us from it. God does not care whether we are the president of a large corporation or a business failure from the world's view. God merely offers the choice. And each time we make even the minutest move in this direction, He rejoices with all His Hosts.

If we choose death, however, be assured we will incarnate somewhere again and again until we feel God's plan — the One Great Law of LOVE. Death is the grave which means more incarnations, more lessons on Earth or elsewhere and eventually another chance to choose life again.

ASCENSION is our predestined purpose. ASCENSION is the evolutionary pathway we are meant to follow. It is the reunion with God, the totality of knowing and loving the Self. But *when* we choose total life, joy and BEingness is up to us.

We need do no more than start with the smallest of prayers. Many ASCENDED ONES wait upon our faintest call to answer with a happy and hearty response. They have stated that less than a tenth of all people in all time periods have ASCENDED. Many of this small percentage came back *after* their death, and with the help of ASCENDED friends, raised their bodies. In the near future they expect a great many more to realize the ASCENDED state. It is the superior choice.

We *can* transmute our bodies. We *can* ASCEND.

Sniff the sweet breath of triumph and supreme happiness. Go forward in the New Vision. . . .

Chapter 2

ONENESS OF FEELING

If we can *feel* at all, we can ASCEND. For *feeling* is the memory of Soul. It is the force that would stabilize and activate into a palpable reality all of our fantasies and interludes. We are here because we choose to *feel*. *Feeling* is the aftermath of etheric energies perceived in the physical body. That being so, the more energy we allow into our physical bodies, the more capable we are of *feeling* with greater intensity.

A *feeling* is our way of knowing that we are animated by the cosmic light energies. The ultimate state of *feeling* is a condition of total joy and alignment with the Father. This would transmute the physical body to light.

Feeling is all there is. Thought and emotion are subcategories of *feeling*. They are only varying degrees or aspects of *feeling*.

A thought is an **organized feeling.** It is a current of varying degrees of *controlled* energy. Conscious thought (organized *feeling*) determines how heavy a substance becomes as it manifests as form. In other words, if the organized *feeling* is to create an item of war, the number of electrons attracted that spin around each atom to produce this crude energy would form metals like iron.

Conversely, if we have lighter, vibrationally more powerful organized *feelings*, we may attract the number of electrons that would spin around atomic nuclei and produce material form that is beneficient. For thought is simply a way that we understand a *feeling* we are having. When we say, "My thoughts are not clear on this or that subject," what we really mean is, "My *feelings* are not clear on this or that subject."

Feeling is never static nor absent. Even though there may be times when we *feel* dead inside, *feeling* is still very much present. *Feelings* can be masked from our conscious awareness by the ego, yet they flow like water within us. *Feelings* can be as deep as a dark subterranean pool, or as quiet as an exposed mountain lake. What we see, hear and smell on this planet is what we and others manifest by our *feelings*.

An emotion is a **rampant feeling**. It is a current of *uncontrolled* energy that courses throughout the body. It is written of old, "What a man thinks, so shall he become." It would be more accurate to say, "What a man *feels* so shall he become." The more thoroughly we condition what we are *feeling*, the more energy we manifest.

Emotions (rampant *feelings*) such as anger, hate, jealousy, greed and fear, cause the atomic elements known as electrons to decentralize from each atom. When this happens, we lose energy. For the electron is an indestructible unit of spiritual force. It is the building block of all form and the energy matrix that supplies the power and light to ASCEND. The spin of the atom is slowed down by any *feeling* less than LOVE!

A strong *feeling* of LOVE causes the atomic center to spin faster and faster, drawing more electrons tighter and tighter into the nucleus. This increases the light, sound and energy of these atoms geometrically and impels an inward tightening centripetal force to self-perpetuate each body atom. If our LOVE is LOVE for God and the true Self as God, then the spin will accelerate until the atom turns into a pure white blinding light — The Fire of ASCENSION.

God is *feeling*. We cannot even say God is a *feeling*. For God in all things is evidenced by all beings and all forms of life — mineral, plant, and otherwise by the *feelings* circulating within those life forms. Therefore, God is the totality of *feeling*.

The "Light of God," as it is called, is generated by the *feeling* that God IS. As we grow and learn through *feeling*, so does the God within us thrust new tendrils into virgin *feeling* territories. For each of us, being slightly different, will express our *feelings* in fresh and diverse ways.

As the *feeling* energy of the true Self flows, we are carried on wings made of the toughest yet lightest material known in any universe — the purest element — the One Great Law of God — LOVE.

Chapter 3

THE GIFT OF SERVICE

The Christ within calls us to serve others at every opportunity. We are uplifted by our willingness. Our reward is greater than joy even though no reward is sought. Acceptance of who and what we are is the place to begin our service. Acceptance equals forgiveness. Once we forgive (accept) ourselves, all doors to heaven open.

Some exercises that may further our role of service are as follows: Look in a mirror and place yourself in the center of the universe. While looking deeply into your own eyes say, "I love you, I love you," several times. See yourself surrounded in a swirl of pure white light while saying this. Or, instead of a mirror, look into your mate's or friend's eyes and say, "I love you." If done enough, this exercise will create a *feeling* within. Practiced daily, this *feeling* will grow, making you more and more mellow and calm. You will smile and be at peace with yourself. And since you are a duplicate of God, you are at peace with God.

Another exercise is to start with body parts. Say to that belly you think is too big, "I love you." If you dislike your belly, those cells composing that part will know this. In other words, you start decaying. The atoms that compose the under-loved part start decentralizing and those particular electrons start returning to the Cosmos. The electron is an indestructible unit of eternal light and energy. The number of these electrons we have is a direct result of how much light and energy we manifest in our life. For this LOVE is the energy that spins the electrons around the nucleus of all atoms.

In this next exercise pretend that there is a small area in back of the heart and talk to that point as though you were speaking lovingly to your own child and say, "Exalted LOVE, manifest thyself within me." Say this over and over directing your attention lovingly at this area behind the heart. Do this throughout the day. At some point there may be a quickening in the heart. This is the physiological response of the heart to more LOVE.

The more we *feel* LOVE, the more we serve others. And there are many ways to serve: Visiting the sick, helping a neighbor build a fence, playing with a child, and aiding or *feeling* kindness toward an injured animal. Even a sincere smile or kind word could be the impetus to lift another out of spiritual lethargy and into a higher consciousness. For the gift of service is the offering of hope. It is not interfering with another's life path. Giving hope simply shows a different perspective.

It offers one a chance to step out of his self-made shackles, and find his own way — the light of God once again glowing in his eyes. Yet we often overlook these minor events when dealing with others. We consider them unimportant. But remember, service without thought of reward is the way to grow in wisdom. And the genuineness of our *feeling* is the only measure which impresses the the Divine Spirit flow.

Accept the Self lovingly and practice the gift of service.

Chapter 4

MYSTICAL PRAYER

Prayer is the focus that creates and sustains all life. The true purpose of prayer is to *feel* our Oneness with God. It is our concentrated beam of self-salvation.

To *feel* the limitless reach of one sincere prayer, envision a pinpoint of pure white light produced by it. An upward spiral then issues from this dot of intense brilliance. As this light widens and expands, the area encompassed is billions of miles across.

There are many ways to pray. Some meditate, some contemplate, and others talk outwardly. What really makes prayer effective is how much *feeling* we generate when saying it. In fact, anything we do that vibrationally elevates *feeling*, is a prayer.

A powerful method for generating this exalted *feeling*, experienced by saints, is Mystical Prayer.

Spend several minutes contemplating your relationship to God. Affirm that you are His child, that you are worthy, and that you have the same power as He. The power of thought and prayer are one. Also the power of His spoken word and your spoken word are one. Ponder these things. Believe them. Drown yourself in these thoughts. Then envision your heart opening and place the heart of Christ within. *Feel* it, know it.

You will begin to *feel* a tingling sensation all around the body. You will *feel* energies building from these thoughts. These tingling sensations will then intensify and you will *feel* chilliness on some parts of the body. Yet on the inside there will be tremendous warmth. Let this warmth flow.

Now, while in that harmonious state express your wish. Do not state it in supplication. State rather, 'Father, I have a need. My need is such...' and then just be. Hold that thought. Hold that *feeling,* for you will *feel* great love and reverence for Self and God. As you hold the thought you will *feel* a portion of the body extending outwards. This is the spirit body. If you keep that thought, you will soon *feel* a oneness with all things. Continue to hold that thought. You may not wish to return to the mundane earth. However, there will come a point at which you must bring yourself back. Because if you stayed, you would *feel* you might explode; for you could not stand any more beauty or joy. At that time speak, 'Amen.' Slowly, you will return to the mundane level. You will *feel* a retraction of the spirit body into the physical. Allow that process to be as it wishes, transpiring in its own time. Do not seek to control it.

Through these *feelings* you will know, without a doubt, something very special has occurred — the way you *truly are* has been felt and recognized.

Pray with *feeling* and *know* that God hears. For no stronger bond can be made with God than by prayer.

Part II

EGO AND ITS MANIFESTATIONS

Chapter 5

THE CUNNING OF EGO

Ego is identification to being only man without realizing that we are also God.

We can recognize the ego because it produces inharmonious *feelings* that make us react. And the ego is cunning. For whenever we forget our Oneness with God, the well-honed handle of this most persuasive tool sets to work. It is composed of all our hurts, fears, connivings, angers, jealousies, lusts, and greeds. It is like a hidden shadow that keeps these traits alive. The ego gives our fears more substance. It flares our frustrations into flames of anger to suit itself because it needs these darker traits.

The ego has constructed an entire energy and life of its own and has been a part of us for so long, that we can scarcely separate the high Soul-Self from the energy-sucking little self. Whenever its sacred den of darkness is threatened, it becomes defensive. It impels us to snarl and growl at our neighbor and the world in order to protect our material and emotional aberrations. It fervently wishes to drag the true Self—Soul, into its lair of webbed complications and petty disputes. Ego is a self-centered, survival-oriented rifle that shoots what doesn't please it and takes advantage of anything that does. It pushes for health or disease according to its self-centered needs. Verily, it deceives so thoroughly that it would make us think we want good for ourselves, while in our heart we secretly harbor our own demise and destruction. For surely will the nightingale's song be snuffed out by ego's craving to own it.

LOVE of the heart is ego's enemy—its ultimate bane. For the true Self is fueled only by LOVE.

Do not liken the true Self to ego for it will be our undoing. Nor struggle with it to gain worth. Instead, liken the true Self to God. Let the plan of ASCENSION naturally unfold.

Next we shall explore the devious faces of ego. . . .

Chapter 6

THE STEALTH OF UNWORTHINESS

The assumption of unworthiness is ego's most insidious creation. It is that slim *feeling* of insecurity or inferiority that makes us *feel* less than God. It is a potent mercenary against ASCENSION and the primary reason most people damage their bodies to the point of death. When we *feel* unworthy we condemn a part of the physical body. Our very chemistry changes and the smell of death exudes from the cells that *feel* too unworthy to live. It is the ultimate in masochism. The actual DNA structures within the cells begin to unravel, short circuiting our loving connection to God. For if we *feel* one pence less than total LOVE in the heart, disruption of our eternal cellular mass occurs. The practice of unworthiness is certain to produce whole body breakdown.

Unworthiness is a phantom. With the stealth of a thief, unwarranted *feelings* of inadequacy slyly surface in the conscious mind. Self-pity and "poor little me" concepts smother the true Self with a blanket of egoic deceit. We think it is correct to abase the Self at the feet of another. We may even *feel* that this false humility is what God wants, that we are *supposed to feel* unworthy.

If we feel less than God, that is — lacking joy, exuberance, inner peace, and enthusiasm, then we are indulging in unworthiness. For as a son and daughter of

God, we are worthy to receive all things, to BE all things. This does not equate with vanity. One who accepts his worthiness can simply BE and there is not a pretentious cell in his BEing, for there is no show to perform. All is within.

Then how do we prevent cellular necrosis as a result of *feeling* unworthy? The answer is to look deeply into the *feelings* and desires in our own hearts.

To *feel* worthy, allow the heart to *feel* happiness, joy, enthusiasm and harmony. Allow the heart to be in LOVE. Allow it to be peaceful and calm.

Radiate happiness of spirit. Sing the name of God always. Soon we become a magnet of ebullient LOVE and our touch becomes as tender as a midsummer night. We leave our old, limited, crucifying *feelings* in the past.

LOVE in the heart, coupled with the power of God, will illumine our footsteps. Observe as the darker energy of enervating pity transmutes into the highest fearlessness of pure white light. Become the poised LOVER of life.

Chapter 7

THE SWAGGER OF VANITY

Vanity lies at the far end of the scale from unworthiness. It is that *feeling* which would make us believe we are actually larger than God by acting superior to others. It is a state of bloated conceit that makes us insensitive to the heartfelt needs of others. We are being vain when we *feel* the need to smash another person's hope or idea underfoot for no other reason than to advance our own. This aggressive, arrogant compulsion occurs craftily in our daily life or it can manifest in a dictatorial thrust that may even rule nations.

Thus vanity is either an obvious or subtle threat to our readiness for ASCENSION. It robs the precious life force by using these energies to maintain a plastic mask.

Watch for these two traps:

1) **Competition -** We *feel* that the only way to stay on an illusionary pedestal is to subjugate or demean those around us — to climb on the backs of others to reach our false position at their expense and then destroy the ladder we forged of energies so that no one can follow.

God does not compete. God only LOVES. This unconditional LOVE is creation itself. To create is to build for others and the Self new ladders to feel ASCENSION.

2) **Fear** - Fear is that which controls our actions when we do not believe that God will take care of our needs. There is fear and self-doubt in both vanity and unworthiness. These two, fear and doubt, are dark flames which fire the ego's vampiric needs.

This understanding of ego, of its two aspects — unworthiness and vanity — should be the foundation of present day studies in psychology. For no matter how severe the case of mental derangement, or what name it is given, it is still ego. It distracts the individual and separates him from the Source — God.

Neither deceptive aspect is necessary. They are only hungry children playing a game of hurt and depression. Feed them with LOVE from the heart. LOVE them into higher light. Teach and tame these twins as we would unruly ones who either demand all of our attention and energy, (i.e. vanity), or sob and moan until we pity them and then give all submissive attention and energy (i.e. unworthiness). LOVE both of these children, for they are misguided cells within us.

Where LOVE is, ego is not.

Chapter 8

THE PASTEBOARD PEDESTALS OF EARTH REALM MASTERS

The pedestal syndrome is another of ego's most clever devices. Ego uses our unworthiness and encourages us to place others above our own God-Self. The self-proclaimed master uses vanity to keep himself on a pedestal. We may even find *ourselves* climbing these cardboard stairs sprinkled with the cheap glitter of vanity, and discover that we can play the guru or master to someone else.

The guru or master may well have started his teaching with a heart full of glowing LOVE. But the seekers, after the master's understanding, push him toward this pasteboard pedestal syndrome. For others have to support this vain illusion. And who better serves this purpose than the seeker who is manifesting his unworthiness?

Unworthiness in a seeker can be as subtle as it is deep. Some masters or gurus will say, "In this teaching there is no worship. Do not worship me, put your attention within." Yet at the same time if these masters or gurus are lecturing somewhere, the earnest seeker striving after something he already has, will be there to partake of the master's holy grail. Many do not realize that their LOVE and attention is what sustains the master/guru at the level of consciousness that he

31

presently operates.

It is almost impossible for one to call himself a 'master,' for the cunningness of ego will fill his cup. The great unworthiness of the well-meaning masses would cast this 'master' in the role of being worshipped regardless of how he actually *feels* about this. This is not to say that it is incorrect to show respect for someone who has truly attained a high understanding of his God Self. All are God.

They might also say, "I am the representative of God and will connect you to the ISness via light, sound, (or whatever)." Or, "I represent the Christ Consciousness." If we are God, what more connection do we need than to realize this? The Christ Consciousness is, always has been and always will be with us. This is not to blast the validity of true teachers and the many wonderful lessons we might learn from them. For a true teacher is one who can allow us to *feel* for ourself. He is not one that always has people goggle-eyed at him. The sincere one might say, "But I *feel* his energy and his sacred handshake lifted me right off the ground!" We never see, hear, smell, taste, or touch anything that we do not already have available to us within our heart center, home of God. If we see lights around the 'guru' it is because we *allowed it within ourself* and not because he induced it by some outer magic. The same goes with sounds or any other manifestations of *feeling*. We are the God that allows this. The master is not giving us some special nectar we do not already have. And if we sustain the contrary thought, however subtly, we become the pedestal syndrome groupie and he becomes the pasteboard pedestal master, deceived by his own devices and fed by the fuel of *our* unworthiness. Looking at life from this viewpoint how can we *not* show respect equally for all life everywhere?

We don't need anyone or anything to make us *feel* worthy to contact our own God-self. Neither will we be doomed to lifetimes of repeated experiences because we don't subscribe to another's philosophies or discourses.

When we LOVE a guru, that LOVE spirals him a little higher. If 50,000 people LOVE the same guru then he is 50,000 times stronger than he was. Invariably the master or guru stays only a notch ahead of his following, spiritually riding their waves of LOVE and devotion ever higher.

When one sincerely seeks greater personal understanding and engages a physical Earth realm master, a curious distortion occurs within the seeker's auric energy patterns. The presence of the energy patterns of the master or guru dimly appears in the seeker's outer aura. If the one who sees this in the aura of the seeker only sees the outer aura and not the Soul vibration in the heart center, the seer may not take any note of this extra load. If, however, the seer could look at the heart center and view the Soul vibration as well, a new perspective might be taken toward the plight of this sincere seeker. For the Soul vibration is the true manifestation of our essence and can be seen in the center of the chest. It comes in through the crown of the head and is the force which animates the body. It expresses personal direction in understanding God.

Thus, when the seeker practices a teaching other than his own, and a so-called Earth realm master is present, the sincere one allows the energy patterns of the master to overlay his own precious heart center. This 'allowed master influence' then becomes a distortion over the heart center of the seeker. It is clouded by the merging of the seeker's heart center with the so-called master presence. This situation can be a useful learning process for the seeker. Every thought, every decision and every desire projected forth in a day's time is colored by this additional prejudice of egoic weight. The seeker will repeatedly say he is free in every sense of the word. He *feels* his path is the highest and most universal the world or any world has ever known. And his master is infallible, the right hand of God. The seeker may even say he does not worship him and his path is totally individual, free of religious dogma.

However, if in his heart, his most sacred *feeling* sanctuary, he has given the smallest fraction of indiscriminate attention to any master or guru, then this could hinder ASCENSION.

In speaking with one of the Beloved ASCENDED ONES, I asked what would be the most important point to make in this chapter. His reply was, "Be your own Master." The implications of these four simple words still ring in my head.

I recall the many belief systems that have enchanted me for many centuries, as well as in this life. I have

34

learned from them all. They helped me to LOVE myself and to *feel* more worthy. If they had not been there throughout the eons of lives, I would have created them, for such was my need. But when I realized the goal of ASCENSION and how it is every man and woman's evolutionary destiny, I began to look at the idols I had loved so long. I looked at the beauracracies, the internal squabbles, and how some fall from favor and others are self-enthroned. I reviewed their ideals and found them all worthy. And I found more. I found the true Self, the GOD I AM, within me. I discovered that if even a billionth of my heart was following the teachings of another physical living guru, I was giving my true Self a slap in the face and limiting the possibilities of ASCENSION. Upon taking an honest look I realized I was scared to leave the security of another's teaching to pursue my true identity. I discovered that no teaching actually advanced me quicker than life itself. And with or without any structured teachings, sooner or later I would have found my own way.

Being one's own Master means more than freeing oneself from some possessive teaching or self-appointed earth master. It means reintegrating the egoic attitudes that held forth the need to seek other teachings, religions, or masters in the first place. It is my opinion that the ASCENDED ONE made that simple statement to me out of great LOVE and compassion to let it be known that in order to enter into Transmutation and ASCENSION we may choose whether *we* are the master of ourself, or someone else is.

INITIATIONS

Another phenomenon of the pedestal syndrome is the rites-of-initiation or some other type of spiritual separation between the members. The one called 'initiate' may say to another, "It doesn't matter that I am a higher initiate than you." Yet secretly, covered by the cunningness of ego, he *feels* superior, a chosen one. The truth is that each person initiates himself when he is ready to do so. For the mask of ego can only drop to reveal another brilliant component of our true Self when we are ready.

And where is the best place to be initiated? . . . .In the living room at home, or a cave in the Himalayas, at Stonehenge, or at Macchu Picchu?

How about a Chinese monastery, or the Hopi Four Corners, maybe through the mail, or by watching Sunday morning T.V.? Why not in a sweat lodge, or by the sage-brush of a female shaman, or a priestess of Isis, the Dalai Lama, or any assorted number of high initiates of this or that movement?

We have a wide range of places. And this list is by no means complete. Think of all the ley lines, which are energy tracings in the earth, and power spots, and vortexes of this or that swirl and color. What grand places to plop our buttocks and wait for revelations to score a hit in the right lobe of the brain. Who knows, even someone dressed like the tooth fairy may arrive to wave us into enlightenment or hand us a holy Oreo cookie to help complete this palliative upliftment.

Do not be fooled by such nonsense. It is fine to visit the places of the past and "ooh and ahh" about their high vibrations and excessive spirituality, for God LOVES us in totality and allows all adventures in any place we wish to be.

We initiate ourselves. The only place we can ever be initiated is within our own heart center. Wherever we happen to be is the appointed place for a personal initiation to occur. For our feet walk on the holiest ground for initiation in existence. Wherever we are, God IS. And wherever God is, any type of initiation is possible. Just take your pick — fire, earth, water — initiation levels one through fifty — twenty-one merit badges — the list is endless.

We are the home of the sacred fire. The AS-CENDED ONES do not care where we are when it's time for our next boot-strap lifting initiation. All they care about is helping us *feel* worthy enough to allow a portion of our ego to be reintegrated with our own aura and thereby further empower ourselves to see the God that we are.

Therefore, let us have fun picking our next initiation site. *Feel* free to choose any of the sixty trillion cells within the physical body to enlighten and emancipate.

Inhale the God that we are and initiate the Self into the ASCENDED states where awaits our dearest friends. The ASCENDED ONES are who and what they are because they have dropped all facades of the ego and nothing blocks them from expressing in fullness their total I AM presence.

The ASCENDED ONES will never limit us. They will never say we must be a celibate or stop eating meat, shave our heads, or avoid anything psychic or pornographic or whatever. They will never say we must chant this or that mantrum. Or that we should follow one spiritual movement or another. They will never tell us to join in groups and project influencing thoughts at another who does not believe what we do in an attempt to bring him around to our persuasion or to lure him back into it if he has left the fold.

The ASCENDED ONES will offer only the message of harmony. This includes all the joy, peace, and enthusiasm they can express to help us snap our shackles and realize through *feeling* that LOVE is all there is.

Chapter 9

THE WORDS OF POSSIBILITY

Our vocabulary is part of the phenomenon that makes us what we are. Words construct the palaces of our innermost desires and bring them to reality. Yet, no word ever truly limits us. It is the way we *feel* about this word in our body that could adversely affect us. Words become the stream that our life fits itself into. What we say we become. What we think we become. What we desire we become.

Ego responds automatically to certain words because they unlock *feelings*. When we actually voice our *feelings* and desires — vibration and form are added. Voice something and it vibrates atomically into a reality that we manifest. The more *feeling* behind the vocalized word, the more powerful that word becomes. This equates to the emotional content.

Many words and phrases are uttered daily without the slightest regard for their effect within the body. When words and speech are used in any other context than to: a) LOVE God; b) LOVE God in ourself; or c) LOVE God in others — then physical and psychological disturbances are the eventual outcome. So, if the *feeling* produced by words is less than LOVE, then the atomic electron spin of certain body atoms begins to slow and gradually the vital electrons (units of eternal light and energy) disperse from us. Finally, the cell that is composed of these altered atoms begins to change its function and begins dying. Medically, this will manifest as some disease process that eventually displaces the body. The results of the following statements are exactingly manifested in our body even though our intent may be innocent. The ideas offered are to help with this understanding. They are *only suggestions*. If we make them into an '-ism or an -ology' then we become the enthralled.

1) I'm afraid that. . .   (Fear is an ego manifes-
   I'm frightened about. . .   tation.)
   I'm scared of. . .

2) I'm angry at or about. . . (Anger and frustration
   Look what you did   are ego manifesta-
   to me. . .   tions.
   I hate. . .

3) I *feel* guilty or he is guilty. . (There is no guilt. This
                                        is stemming from the
                                        ego manifestation of
                                        unworthiness.)

4) I think he's an old 'so   (Judgment. We lower
   and so'. . .   our own vibration and
   She/he *should* be. . .   destroy our physical
                                body when we judge
                                others.)

5) I'm worried about...
   I'm nervous about...

(All tensions denote a lack of LOVE for Self and others. This is an energy-losing, body destroying proposition. There is no worry.)

6) That's evil...

(There is no evil. Those darker brothers who would lead us in a lesser light simply haven't learned the lessons of LOVE. They have forgotten our common goals - Transmutation and ASCENSION. We allow them entrance into our life by our own words and thoughts. We attract what we say.)

7) That's impossible...
   It's impossible for...
   Be realistic...

(We choose our limits. The One Great Law has no boundaries.)

8) I want...
   I can't...
   I'm tired (of)...

(These statements denote lack, limitation and separation. They do not exist in God.)

41

9) I've got to. . .or have to. . . (This speech pattern is typical of an obsessive-compulsive situation. Watch for it. Either or both of these can limit the amount of light entering the body.)

10) *ALL* curse words or derogatory words. . . (Everytime we say them we harshly condemn ourself, even if in jest or jokes. For they vibrationally key deep *feelings*. The Soul remembers many of these words from their misty origins when helplessness and a draining depression of lost hope were experienced. These particular *feelings* are stored physically in the primitive brainstem. Their constant use, even naively, will manifest a myriad of emotional and physical problems. There is no way to condemn others without condemning ourself.)

42

11) I like you *but*. . .

('But' limits or completely negates the statement which preceded. Substitute 'and' for 'but.' 'And' is inclusive. It is full of possibility.)

12) I don't know. . .

(If we continuously feed this concept, even casually, into the cellular structure of the body, it will shut out more and more "knowingness" about everything. Then what if we really don't know something? If this is stated, even by inference, no matter how mundane or arcane it is, we continue to limit ourselves. "I don't know" is a death admission. Rather, we "know" all because all is available through our auric field which is interconnected with all that is known, spoken,

thought, or created.
We are God and God
knows.)

As an interesting game, carry a pen and paper around and each time you say "I don't know," mark it on the paper no matter what the context of the conversation. Count how many times you have stated this at the end of the day. Do this for one week, then eliminate, "I don't know" for one week. Watch how your entire behavior patterns change. It will surprise you. Consider using this instead, "I know and am not remembering it right now." Simply choose to *know*.

Another group of statements that create confusion are those which use the term 'unconscious.' We are never 'unconscious.' This is another fine term that ego has concocted. It automatically blocks us from *feeling* the One Great Law of God. We may be unaware about aspects of a certain subject, thing or part of our emotional Self but that is a far cry from being 'unconscious.' Unconsciousness presupposes death and death is an unnecessary occurrence.

Here's another favorite - 'subconscious.' I have played for years with this one. What an ingenious trap. Nothing is hidden behind the misty veil of 'subconscious' as it is called. This is another death mechanism. People shirk in fear from the hideous face of what they think might emerge from deep inside themselves.

We are conscious of everything, all the time! It is

only *our choice* to remain unaware of certain aspects of this ONENESS. God did not initially create a subconscious - *we* did.

We can free ourselves of these destructive parasites simply by releasing these terms. Work from the premise that we are totally aware of all. In order to *feel* and experience the Transmutation and ASCENSION stages — choose consciousness.

Words should be our servants. With undisciplined usage they become enslavers. Until we are habitually aware of the effect words have upon us, it is better to utilize only those that are energy producing and body building. Words that tighten and increase the atomic electron spin for more light and power within are:

I AM. . .

I LOVE . . .

I CHOOSE . . .

I LIKE . . .

I KNOW . . .

I WILL . . .

I CAN . . .

Start your sentences with these and see what happens. You will have re-patterned and re-tooled the threads of communication.

Let ASCENSION be the only purpose of speech.

Part III

THE INTERCONNECTEDNESS OF LIFE

Chapter 10

THE SYNCHRONIZATION OF BEINGNESS

We are interconnected to the motion of an atom spinning on the far side of the most distant star in the universe. And every personal atom is the gravity for every realm. We are the point of ultimate centeredness. The essence of each point in space is the blueprint of our body.

Along a line of past and future, we are the architect, the building moment of every foundation. The curves of the galaxy are the wrinkles in our skin and the smooth gloss of the moon is our shiny fingernails.

All matter and all thoughts of matter are our blood. They flow through the vesseled corridors of our time and space and seep through those walls melding with the fantasies of our sweetest slumber. Climb into a tree and we find we are its trunk and branches, the knots and bark that squirrels feast upon. It is our lips that the clouds touch in the bronze dawn of forever. And it is our kiss that awakens the deepest sleeper to know about LOVE.

God is the great interconnector, the Absolute I AM, the ISNESS of weavings and looms yet unimagined. And in this Wholeness, God anoints us. We are the conduit for eternity.

The breathing of our smallest sigh is the answer God has waited for. We are the ALL in ALL. There is not a single event that we do or don't do, no matter how infinitessimal, that is not *felt* in all realms and beyond in past, present and future. We are the forceful fist that can rip through the veil of ignorance. For to think we are limited by time and space is an illusion for sheep and worshippers of sheep.

It is entirely possible that we are already working as an ASCENDED ONE in the future with those in that future time who desire to know more about the AS-CENSION process. Or we may be working in the past as a teacher to someone. As there is only the NOW, so there is only this moment to live in all times.

An ASCENDED teacher and friend provides and example of this. I first encountered him while working with someone on a health problem. This ASCENDED ONE appeared as an old Mayan medicine man. Several months later he appeared again as a young man dressed like a prosperous 17th century gentleman. When questioned about this, he stated that he knew the man with the physical problem when they were Mayans and that he could better accept that energy frequency. He appeared to me as he was when he ASCENDED because he knew I could relate to *that* frequency better. He was both personalities. Both sightings on my part were real. One dealt with a past in which he hadn't ASCENDED and the other when he had ASCENDED. Yet they were occurring at the same time.

He was, is, and always ASCENDED. So it is with everyone. For all is happening at once in this very moment even as our eyes follow the line on this page.

Time and space are grandiose illusions. For LOVE is the interconnecting link that allows us to BE whatever, whenever, however and as much as we want to BE. The total of all intersections of all matter and the *feelings* generated by these intersections–is LOVE.

If a sparrow falls on the other side of the planet, we *feel* it. If a man gets a grain of sand in his eye on the other side of the planet we *feel* his discomfort. And when he takes that same grain of sand out of his eye, we *feel* his relief. All universes and beyond are connected. They breathe in one breath.

Universal knowledge is not unattainable. The first step is to realize that we have access to all there is because **WE ARE ALL THERE IS!** In the pulsating heart center of our greatness, calmly swirls the reason and the answer. Acknowledge that WE ARE HERE TO LOVE and from this, all interconnections we wish to know — past, present or future — are illumined by the brilliance that emanates from our LOVING heart.

To interconnect with all life we do but one thing: Acknowledge, again and again, the One Great Law of God — the most complete synchronization of BEingness.

Chapter 11

CYCLES OF TIME

Definition of the
Pythagorean Master Number 11

THE LIGHT BEARER

*One is seen as an indivisible individual
with his two centers joined. His time bound
consciousness spirals toward fulfillment in
the true reality of God. Great light radiates
outward from this Knowable Unity.*

God has created a lattice network upon which we
may swing to and fro like an industrious spider. This intricate web is called Time. The oneness of the moment
separates into billions of parts so that we may be able
to relate to the experiences we have in time segments.
But all things happen *at once*.

Understanding this portion of the Interconnectedness of life is elementary. Time is simply not real from
the perspective of the One Great Law. Although time
seems so definite in this universe, it is only a limited
piece of reality. Like all pieces, the whole is contained
within each one, as parts of a shattered hologram still
contain the total picture. We use the constructed il-

lusion of moments in the past and future so that we can hang our *feelings* (pleasant or not) upon a definite time rung. Should we relate back to a rung of *feeling* in the past and bring that *feeling* once again into the present moment, we have an opportunity to resolve and take the mishandled energy upward into total knowingness.

We have a past, present and future. Within each of these is also a past, present and future. Schematically, we might represent it thus:

Diagram 1

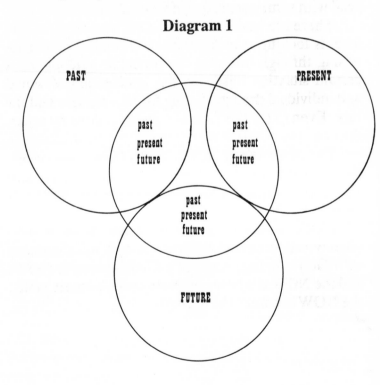

Notice that each circle interconnects the other. View these in a deeper perspective as spheres. Each past, present, and future sphere has within it a separate past, present, and future of its own.

Future prediction is a tricky business. These spheres roll along in a cyclical manner and can alter at any moment in any direction. This may change the outcome of a would-be situation that is destined to happen one month from now. However, futures can be read with some accuracy and pasts altered.

There are Master Futures. One who views at this level is looking at all available eventualities and surmising through intuition the probable outcome of a certain situation based on the intersection of world and individual thought-*feeling* forms — present and future. Even today this type of viewing is done by some. An example of this level of viewer was Nostradamus.

The more we get in touch with these time cycles, the more our personal timing becomes accurate and we start seeing pasts and futures. For time is consciousness itself.

God's timing is totally conscious. What is mistakenly called unconsciousness is only misalignment with God's timing. And since God's timing is NOW, and the NOW is where complete consciousness exists, the NOW becomes the eternal.

Chapter 12

THE PRINCIPLE OF WITHIN-NESS

When defining the God within, I am choosing the phraseology of the All-Powerful I AM Ubiquity. For there are few ways better to understand what God is than to think of IT in the statement — I AM. Being an Ubiquity, means that one is tied into an everywhereness and everythingness that one wishes to know or BE through *feeling*.

This Ubiquity is recognized *within* ourselves at the heart center. It contains all the *feelings* of joy and elation we will ever need to transmute and ASCEND the physical body.

A clear "touch" to the heart center produces a *feeling* of upliftment and revitalization that can be gained whenever desired. It is the "knowing," through *feeling*, that I AM God. Through this link, one can see, hear, smell, taste, levitate, transmute, and ASCEND. We can know and BE in any place, any time, or in all places simultaneously if we wish.

The principle of Within-ness is as subtle as it is simple. Most spiritual teachings I have been involved with say, "Go within." Intellectually, I understood this. Diligently I practiced a prayer/meditation/contemplation at least twice a day of 30 minutes or longer. I used techniques, mantrums, white lights, blue lights, sounds, smells. . .and many times did touch aspects of this All

Powerful I AM Ubiquity. Yet, I still *felt* unworthy to consider it all me. Rather, I assumed that these *feelings* were being sent to me or that I drew them into me from my gurus or from the flow of spirit. The surprise came when I realized I already *had* the *feelings* and was drawing *nothing* from the outside.

The ego has created the illusion which keeps us looking outside ourselves for personal truth and guidance. We get sidetracked by the subtlety of a *feeling* that there is still some spirit flow (prana), some person, object, sound, some thing *outside* that provides the magic needed to complete ourselves. *Nothing* is outside of us, especially God.

Our true spiritual home is where we *feel* from. It is the end of our fingers. It is the brush of our hair against the breeze. It is every *physical* cell within the body that expresses itself as *feeling*. This could be a touch, a pressure, a burning, an aching, or a titillation of great pleasure.

An exercise is given to help experience this.

It is suggested that quiet time be spent each day, preferably in the early morning. Choose a comfortable chair, close your eyes and sit as long as you like. God doesn't have a clock! I usually sit at least 30 minutes at a time, twice a day. It is not unusual, however, for me to stop after only 5 minutes, or to remain for an hour. Gauge yourself according to your *feelings* rather than structured dogma about what you think you must do to *feel* God. Each of you will do it differently. So much the better.

Envision your entire body as being white light. See its beams coming from you in all directions. After you have pictured this, sense what this whiteness *feels* like. There are no measurements for perception. Just relax and *feel*. Remember, there is no trying. There is only doing and no one is judging what you do. God doesn't carry measuring sticks. God just IS. Say a word of thanks to God for allowing you to be completely surrounded in white.

Next envision your heart center. (See Diagram 2.) This is where you and God are in partnership. See this also as being brilliant white. Then, off to the side of this brilliant heart center, envision a two dimensional mesh of fine woven, dark cloth floating above your solid white center like a black cloud. This cloud is the ego. It is the great distractor. Now, see yourself going underneath, around, or through it so that you maintain centeredness. Totally merge yourself with it. Every single beam of the heart center's brilliant light is resonating with all parts of the infinite dimensions of ASCENSION. Finally, to "seal the pact" between you and God breathe an affirmation such as, "I and the Father are ONE." You may state this anyway you like: "I am One with God," or "I am God now," or "Thank you God." Remember you are *not* speaking out to God. You are *already* where God is. . .within.

Diagram 2
HEART CENTER

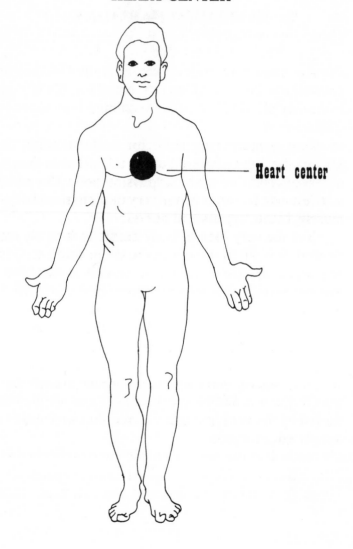

Heart center

Chapter 13

MAXIMUM HARMONY

All awareness of the spiritual life is found in the physical life. All awareness of the physical life is found in the spiritual life. We are in Maximum Harmony with God when all sixty trillion of our body cells are pure. If we want a measuring stick for understanding our spiritual Self and where we are in this process, then we observe the way we treat our physical body. **The mystic is within our bones. It is our very own physical body — muscle, blood, organs and nerves.**

Yet the very idea of body harmony is rarely considered. It is *felt* that one can do, say or think anything one wishes without the least inkling of what those bombshells of discordant *feelings* are doing to the body. So we allow our thoughts and *feelings* to run amuck like madmen in the streets. Eventually these unrestrained *feelings* shatter windows and destroy the very heart of our downtown body area.

We become weak and our immune system starts breaking down. Illness overcomes us and we are consumed by the very *feelings* of havoc that we created in untutored ignorance.

Body cells are never unconscious or subconscious. They have levels of awareness in relation to each other. Those *in* harmony, we *feel* and are aware of. Those *moving into* harmony, we are beginning to *feel*. Those *moving away* from harmony we do not *feel,* for their physiological functions are lowered. This does not mean these latter cells are totally unconscious. It means these particular cells are simply more unaware of the unifying process going on in the rest of the system.

Inharmony within any particular body cell increases the amount of tension around the cell membrane, increases acid production, and reduces the amount of oxygen utilized by the cell. The degree of relaxation throughout the body equates exactly with the number of cells that are receiving proper nourishment and growth. These nourished cells can prosper and clone themselves. Oxygenation is increased because of correct outer membrane resistance, proper acid-alkaline balance, and correct elimination of cell waste acids.

A way to know when we are moving toward Maximum Harmony is by experiencing a certain *feeling* — best described as a vibration that occurs through the entire body. From teaching classes and talking to people about Maximum Harmony, it is my belief that this *feeling* happens occasionally to many and is usually spontaneous. It most often starts in the morning between the states of dreaming and fully awakening. Some report that it *feels* like a buzzing or humming throughout and is exceedingly pleasant.

This *feeling* can be most easily induced by the practice of mystical prayer as is described in Chapter 4.

Joy, peace, enthusiasm, happiness, and genuine laughter also create these *feelings* as well as an environment of relaxation. Maximum Harmony leads the body into total integration with God.

Chapter 14

ATTUNEMENT OF THE SENSES

There is only one true sense — *feeling*. The simplicity of this is startling in its application. We automatically increase the sensitivity levels of sight, sound, smell, and taste as we increase the *feeling* of LOVE for ourself. This quickens the body vibrations and tunes us to other levels.

SIGHT

This sense is enhanced by what is known as auric vision. First, we can see with the third eye alone. This means that we view the aura internally. Outer color does not appear to the physical eye. Secondly, we can actually view with the physical eyes, the outer color pattern around the person. Ideally, a complete synthesis of the two methods is desirable.

Everyone can attune to both methods. It is the ego construct of unworthiness that keeps telling us, "I can't see auras. Others can but not I." **All can see**.

Increased sight may begin with flashes of light to the side of our field of vision. These can range from pinpricks to rather large flashes. When praying or meditating with eyes closed, we may see these flashes more directly in front of us. When talking or sitting with eyes open we may view them out of the corners of our

63

eyes. They will often be different colors and shapes.

Some schools of thought say these flashes are masters, teachers or guides showing themselves to us. This may be so. More often than not, however, these flashes of light are our assurance that we can, and most of the time have, touched another dimension with our *feeling* of sight. The vibration we are all connected with, that appears as a pinprick of white light, is the Christ Consciousness.

Seeing the aura with the outer eyes could easily happen through increasing *feeling* power which activates more rods in the eyes. (Rods are a part of the anatomy of the physical eye).

There are various techniques for achieving auric vision. This is my favorite:

1) Be seated in a chair with a solid white wall or screen opposite you, so that who or whatever you are looking at will have this as a background.

2) The eyes and the muscle groups around them must be very relaxed. To help with this, do the following: Close your eyes and open them very slowly, looking at the person or object. Do this at least twenty times thinking of sleepily relaxing your eyelids while raising them. This should relax the eyes sufficiently and allow more rods to begin functioning.

3) Light a candle. Candlelight is about the best medium for seeing the colors of the aura. These colors
are vibrationally similar to fire.

4) Partially darken the room.

5) Hold the candle between you and the person to
whom you are looking. Move the candle around to
different positions close to the head of the obser-
vee.

6) Look for the outlines of the auric field. Look for
shapes and any color you may see.

Do this daily, preferably before going to bed, for 15
minutes or longer. If done diligently, the outlines of the
outer aura may begin to appear and colors may follow.

HEARING

Don't underestimate the potency of this sense and
the appropriate tuning of it. Have you ever awakened
in the middle of the night in a room where there was
complete silence and heard a high-pitched hum in your
ears? You may have discounted it thinking it to be your
blood pressure. Rather, you were probably hearing your
own sound and its connection to *your own* universes. If
you would take time to be still and listen you would be
rewarded.

1) When in your quiet time, with eyes closed, listen for

a humming sound and subsequent changes as you relax. Become aware of changes; listen to the highs, lows, and subtle differences in pitch and timber. At work or play, listen for these sounds.

2) Notice their tone, the richness, the dissonances. You can use this modality of sound to alert you to what is happening in different situations. When it suddenly changes be aware that something is happening which could affect you. This sound is not coming from outside you, for **all** is within. If you hear high buzzing, flutes, bees, thunder, or whatever, and this increases, that is good. You are getting closer to the heart center. You are becoming more aware of them as you approach your union point with God. You *are* the universe you hear—just as you *are* the universe you *feel*. You vibrate to all the Realms of Transmutation. The ISness can produce anything, any sound.

Be wary though, for if there is nothing else to make abeyance to, the ego will let you scrape your belly to the Spirit Flow itself, allowing you to believe that it comes into you from outside.

SMELL AND TASTE

Since there are no limits to the All-Powerful I AM Ubiquity, you can experience the accentuation of smell and taste to any extent you wish. A misunderstanding found in many spiritual teachings is that smell and taste drop away after a certain point in its evolution. This is simply not so. How could you lose anything if it is **within** you? If you can smell and taste now, it is not logical to assume that these senses would disappear later. Your entire physical body ASCENDS.

I have met several people who are quite aware of smells that are not within the normal range of olfaction. I have also met those who get a taste in their mouth that clues them into what is happening with another person or place without having eaten anything. The more you LOVE, the more your body becomes conscious. Smell then could be extended to any part of your BEingness, even into the next realm. Exercises for smell and taste can be performed similar to the one for hearing. Tune into that faculty while in your quiet period and allow yourself to smell and taste the nuances around you. Remember: these too are extensions of *feeling.*

SLEEP

Sleep is actually a sense, although not usually thought of in this category. The Soul is using this time to *feel* and experience the other realms of our birthright.

Allow the body at least 7 to 8 hours of sleep if possible. A nap after the midday meal is not an indication of weakness as many believe. It is good to rest after lunch for 15 to 30 minutes as this follows the health cycles of the body and prepares it for a more productive afternoon and evening.

LOVE is the omnipotence within all of your senses, and your senses will be honed to a razor-sharp perfection as you approach your inevitable evolutionary destiny. Upon having totally cleaned and cleared yourself, every cell of you can see, hear, smell and taste. For *feeling* is now complete.

See with your heart. Smell with your toes. Hear with your fingers. Taste with your hair. The ASCENDED ONES become what they wish with no physical poisons to limit their senses. At this very moment this same ASCENDED future floats within the organelles and mitochondria of your cellular NOW.

Chapter 15

REALMS AND BROTHERHOODS OF LIGHT

A realm is a place vibrating at a rate our physical eyes do not see. These varying bands of vibration are all around us, interconnecting us through *feeling*. Just as the band of vibration we see produces this world and physical universe, so do the multiple bands of vibration that we do not see produce countless universes and worlds.

The realms still exist within a framework of time, space and matter and can greatly alter from realm to realm. They are our honing ground, our razor-edged tightrope that allows us to walk and fall, walk and fall, as often as is necessary as we approach our evolutionary destiny.

The realms are twelve in number and within each of those are subdivisions of frequencies called dimensions. There are twelve dimensions in each realm. All total, there are 144 dimensions.

Each of these dimensions and realms is a paradise of knowledge. They are like an accordion with 144 dimensions that are pumped in and out by the hands of God.

Reference points constantly change in the realms. As the color of light changes in a rainbow, so do the vibrations in the multi-faceted realms. Every chart or drawing of the realms is different from the other. This is not to say that astral, causal, and other etheric heavens do not exist. They do. It is that we as individuals experience and harmonize with them in different ways from each other because of our particular biochemistries. The authors and gurus of these different charts were seeing and experiencing the way their own body cells were aligned with light.

The difference between the first realm and the twelfth realm is that in the first realm things are thicker. Otherwise, consciousness is consciousness. And we can be just as spiritually conscious on the first realm as on the fourth or the twelfth. It all depends upon where we choose to exist in order to gain more experience.

For example, at present we are in the twelfth dimension of the fourth realm. The fact that planet Earth is not in a higher realm vibrationally does not matter. For we chose this realm and dimension to express our God-Self this time. We chose this moment to learn and complete the ASCENSION. We chose to open the heart center and **BE** the One Great Law.

Those inhabiting the first realm are not necessarily rocks as some would have us believe. Instead there are millions of wondrous planets, peopled by millions of interesting folks. Some of them look just as human as we do. Some of them live in houses and have vehicles and pay bills to phone companies just as we do. Some of them have just as many hassles and glories to uplift and learn in their times. All life everywhere has equal chance to choose the materials it wishes in order to learn

70

the One Great Law.

The sooner we realize that spiritual advancement is a matter of FREE WILL, the easier it will be for us to accept that life everywhere is similar. **We are joined together by our similarities, not our differences.** And there is one quite unmistakable similarity. That is — LOVE.

We are the light-bearers, the Master-builders, and the ASCENDED ONES. We can use the realms and Brotherhoods to our advantage to help learn this.

What is a Brotherhood? It is a grouping of Souls with a common purpose working toward a certain goal. There are different types of these. In this manual I refer principally to two Brotherhoods — the Brotherhood of Intuition and the White Brotherhood. They are groupings of very aware Souls whose desires are to bring greater light to this and other planets seeking harmony. They are universal helpers of God.

All the Brotherhoods of Light extend their earnest hand to take us into shining consciousness if we just ask. They are single-mindedly committed to the One Great Law and to make us aware of the same.

Remember the statement from our holy writ: "It is your Father's good pleasure to give you the Kingdom." *Luke 12:32.* The Kingdom spoken of begins with our understanding of the realms, our place therein and our inevitable evolutionary destiny into the next stage.

Chapter 16

BROTHERHOODS AND FORCES OF CONFUSED PURPOSE

This concept can be a great stumbling block. We often *feel* afraid of dark brotherhoods or negative energies and thus draw them to us. Changing this attitude is needed.

Of course negative energies, dark brotherhoods, devils and such do exist. Just as those places of lesser light such as Hell exist in order to house those of confused purpose. Having traveled over most of this fine planet and visited many others, I have seen situations more heart rending than a fiery pit. Although there *are* Souls who choose to spend time in such environs, these are only darker places where the One Great Law of God is not as fully manifested.

Have you ever been in a cave and *felt* afraid in the darkness, in the absence of light? Was God not in the cave too? In fact, God is the cave as well. If we choose to gain our lessons about LOVE in darker areas for awhile, this is allowed. Our *real* fears of these dark places are the locked-in cellular body toxins which block light. They are not just fears of Beezelbub or such named forces of terror. Instead, they are the barely awakening body cells that are just beginning to spin with greater frequency.

For every dark place within the body is an unaware

cell or cell aggregate. Demons, dark brotherhoods, and malevolent entities are only attracted to us through these particular cells of our body in which an inharmonious *feeling* is present. These cells are so clogged and vibrationally different that we may not even *feel* that portion of the physical body. And when they are cleared it is like becoming aware of our left arm for the first time.

Darkness exists only within certain portions of the realms. Each of these realms is vibrationally represented within some cellular portion of our own body; when we generate a field of fear and doubt, we are vibrating with these darker elements. Can other persons of lesser light hurt us? Not unless we let them. God is always protecting us if we ask. And ask we must. For not asking is the little self, the ego, vying for power.

The brotherhoods of lesser light are seeking more light just as we are. They are doing it by means of force, thievery, and vampirism. However, if we stay connected to our source by acknowledging God, no harm or vampirism will assail us. Neither can any devils nor mischief makers bother us. Yet when we do allow them in our life, we can choose to learn from them. They help us to face our fears and all the limiting, reactive ego states we harbor in our hearts. They are part of our self-directed learning program.

The attacks made by those of darker purpose can be recognized. There is a general fatigue, loss of appetite, weight loss, confusion, sleeplessness or nightmares, bruises and sometimes an occasional difference in body odors.

There are also subtler invasions. In many ways they are more injurious. These types of manipulations (i.e. black magic) are done by those living here who employ techniques fostered by the dark brotherhoods to gain control of others for their own nefarious intent.

The saddest part of this odious game is that the dark brotherhoods are only fulfilling their own sinister desires by working through those who are naive and misled. And in doing so, not only do they gain the satisfaction they crave, but also *draw the actual life force from the person they are guiding as their channel.*

So the willing human participant in this role of confused purpose loses twice. First, he loses whatever energies he has siphoned off from victims he manipulates. Second, he loses portions of his own life energies to those in the dark brotherhoods. He is then only an intermediate vampire who gains and *feels* this stolen energy for a brief time before having to pass it on to those whose greed is greater than his. The illusive gain felt is only a slight energy boost as the energies coerced from another pass through, feeding his frenzy, and giving a fleeting *feeling* of elation and power.

Some of these devious techniques are fostered in mind control schools. This is not to say that the study of mind control is not beneficial. It is. The problem occurs when these techniques are practiced in order to wrest from another some advantage without consent. Some of these sinister approaches even appear to be wholesome on the surface. Beware—for they are not.

Especially those who *teach* these techniques, are setting themselves up for painful experiences either later in this life or certainly in those following.

Let this be the yardstick. If any teaching promotes other than LOVE and personal freedom for the Soul, it is leading down a rocky path strewn with the boulders of ego.

What good are short-term material gains, when our very Soul is made to pay the note? What benefit is the enslavement of another's body for sexual lust in this life when the payment in future lives may demand the same or worse? What would be gained by coercing another to think as we do when these aberrant attitudes will be the death of our physical form?

Then what if we *feel* we are already the victim of one of these subtle attacks from the hands of dark teachers? Realize first that we invited this lesson at the ego level of unworthiness or vanity. Next, enter into humble and sincere prayer asking for freedom from this yoke. See the Self surrounded in white light and declare that we are living our life only in the pure light of the One Great Law of LOVE.

If we know our assailant in this game, pray that he, too, sees the clear light and wish him always the best with as joyous *feeling* as can be mustered.

If we do not know our assailant, then pray that whoever it may be receive the exuberance of pure light, see for himself his confusion and end his dangerous ploys. Pray for these confused brothers just as earnestly as we would for ourself.

Light is FOREVER. Darkness is temporal — concerned only with time and space.

Purify the old fears of *feeling* controlled by dark forces. These are ego constructs from the past. LOVE those dark confused ones who persecute. Look toward the light of FOREVERNESS within and *feel* connection with the One Great Law.

If this be done, protection and Soul advancement are gained... "and we shall live in the house (our physical body) of the Lord forever. . . Amen."

Chapter 17

THE PERFECT ETHERIC DOUBLE

The perfect etheric double is a gift from God that allows us to experience freedom in a total way. For our interconnectedness encompasses all our bodies on all realms.

The perfect double is made of 360 perfectly white cycles which create a form that looks like us in every detail. Even if a part of the physical body has been maimed or lost in surgery, the perfect double will not show this loss. The word "perfect" implies just that. If the gallbladder be surgically removed, the perfect double will still have one. Viewed aurically, the missing organ is seen as complete. It is the etheric double that keeps the body functioning in that organ area.

The perfect double then, is essential to our very existence. It gives us the freedom to explore in greater depth this universe and any other. It allows the *feeling* experience that leads to a total process of BEing.

Occasionally a seer viewing the double, mistakes it for a partially complete etheric sheath. The double is not just an etheric sheath. And not all etheric sheaths are complete. Extended sight which is not limited to only two or three dimensions, reveals the perfect double to be slightly off center of the physical body. That is why it is sometimes so hard to distinguish.

The perfect etheric double is one of our best friends in our quest for the hand of the Most High. It is a perfect part of our spiritual anatomy. It is ourselves in our most handsome moment at any age we wish.

Chapter 18

OVERSOULS AND SIMULTANEOUS EXISTENCE BODIES

Oversouls are etheric bodies that are connected to each other by a strong rope-like cord. In the 4th realm we are connected both to the 5th realm body and the 3rd realm body. The cord carries through the 12th realm, connecting our Oversouls with the Heart of God. As a Soul, we can express and establish as many temporary etheric sheaths as we wish and wherever we wish. That is, there can be several bodies in one realm.

God is the principal Oversoul. Next is the Christ, which is God's first manifestation. From that point are decatrillions of Oversouls, each with its own cord extending from the Heart of God all the way to the 1st realm. We are *literally* connected to God, not just figuratively. We are an extension of God, given Free Will, to develop our own personality, ego, and set of experiences as Soul. We and our Oversouls, as collective fragments, are like separate beads along a string.

These parts of ourselves are some of the most true and loving friends we will ever meet. They are aspects of us that exist in the other realms. They are separate personalities however, and like us, they are learning to *feel* the One Great Law. Some have mastered their ego self and are helping many as they continue to grow in the infinite light of God.

How does one recognize an Oversoul? This can and does happen in a variety of different ways tailored to each individual. Oversouls are part of us and we part of them. As more awareness is gained we will be made very aware of them. They may be present when we least suspect, and be responsible for giving that extra little nudge or intuition to go forward with an idea.

While dreaming we often encounter one of our Oversouls that exists in another realm. Recognizing them is usually not too difficult because they tend to look a great deal like us. Generally, there is an even split between the number of male and female Oversouls that we have in our particular grouping.

This situation exists because there are male and female aspects that require attitudinal balance within the total Soul Self for a full understanding of LOVE. Sooner or later we will meet one or all of our Oversouls. As we become aware of being in another realm, be certain that at least one of our Oversouls is close by. We can also request a meeting before going to sleep each night and see what happens.

Another way to meet these Oversouls is through a physically living person who channels the presence of another. In these days and times more and more of the Great White Brotherhood are stepping forward and speaking through physically embodied people in order to spread the truth about the One Great Law. However, we must determine for ourself the validity of these channels and the sources who speak through them. Questions we might ask are: 1) Specifically identify themselves; 2) Are they committed to only the highest and best in and of the Christ in each individual; 3) Do they open their discussion with a prayer before they speak of anything else?

Lastly and always go by your *feelings*. Does it *feel* harmonious? If it does, fine. If it does not, dismiss it. Ask, "Are they expressing through *feeling* the One Great Law?"

The crucial time in which we are living is the main reason we see and hear so much of this channeling activity. It is the end of a great cosmic cycle and the beginning of a new time.

The Christ Consciousness is moving through the realms quickly and the totally devoted Brotherhoods are doing all they can to prepare this planet to go forward instead of backward as it has in the past.

One of the methods in which I became aware of my Oversouls was by talking to them as though they were there, even though I could not see them at that time. This is an admirable habit that many are often ridiculed for. If we don't think the room we are reading this manual in is occupied by others besides ourself in nonphysical bodies, we are mistaken. Be certain that most of the time our friends are with us in a form unseen by the physical eyes but are present nevertheless. So it is a good, solid, first step toward meeting our friends, guides and Oversouls to address them as though they were there in the room.

Stretch out with *feelings* while talking to them. Let

whatever we *feel* register within. It may be a shiver or an increase in the sound in our ears or a peaceful *feeling* of warmth and acknowledgment. Many have doubts and fears about doing this, which is the ego blocking. To *feel* more comfortable say a prayer and bless whatever is *felt* and ask in the name of GOD and the Christ for only the highest and best in life — that whoever we are talking to is of the Christ light. Then talk away, certain that they are listening too.

If something happens to terminate our body *or* the bodies of one of our Oversouls, then a group decision amongst all Oversouls is made as to where the Soul particle will next reincarnate.

GRAND OVERSOULS

A Grand Oversoul is one who is responsible for many oversouls. An example of this is the Grand Oversoul of all Inanimate Objects. This means such things as chairs, tables, couches, toys, TVs, houses, rocks, cars, papers, etc. These objects are generally not given much consideration.

They are found in some form in every realm. Yet they are in the fourth realm and all other realms as servants of all races and civilizations. By mutual agreement we consent to have these in our particular orbits.

Just as we have a heart center which is our connection point to God, so does every single inanimate object, piece of object, and even what we consider as trash in our immediate radius. Therefore, as it is our inevitable evolutionary destiny to ASCEND, so is it theirs.

In fact, one of the most interesting experiences of my life was meeting an ASCENDED ONE from a planet populated mostly by machines. Before ASCENSION, he wore a machine form. This astounded me as I was limited at that time to thinking that only what I considered "conscious" beings could ASCEND. Inanimate objects in all realms are conscious in their own way with their own heart center and methods of improving themselves through *feeling*.

In a dream when we find ourselves surrounded by inanimate objects it is important that we recognize these as living. Touch them and *feel* their solidity.

Then what about familiar objects such as the chair we are sitting in at this very moment? We desire and wish for certain objects. Desires and wishes are *feelings*. When enough *feeling* is manifested, the envisioned object is magnetically drawn into our radius. Conversely, *feelings* of unworthiness keep us from physically manifesting other objects, like furniture and cars. Then we lament about lack of money.

The ASCENDED ONES have taught that money is another form of *feeling*. It is the exchange of our precious energies that we exert in labor, for a medium that could represent this. The greater the *feeling* of worthiness and LOVE of Self, the more we manifest by multitudes of various avenues. If we would LOVE money with our heart center and spend it joyously to pay debts and buy groceries, we may notice some interesting results in daily life. As we LOVE, we release. As we release, we flow. As we flow, unworthiness cannot find a niche in consciousness.

Inanimate objects are like pets. They exist as they do by choice to teach us LOVE. They serve and ask only LOVE in return. And by LOVING them for what they are, we are also LOVING ourselves for what we are.

SIMULTANEOUS EXISTENCES

Another crucial understanding is knowing what constitutes a simultaneous-existence-body and how the perfect double produces it.

When we dream, we often create a body that can look like us in another realm for our use that night. This solid, yet temporary creation can be any age, shape, or sex. This replica, called a simultaneous-existence-body, acts as our tendril to *feel* what we need at that time.

It is created in this manner. We have a desire. Desire is *feeling. Feeling* is energy. This energy is the clay that awaits our mold. The mold is our perfect double. When we wish to experience a *feeling* in dreaming, the perfect double molds a replica of us.

When we awaken from sleep, this extended, solid body, dematerializes and returns into our physical body as expanded *feeling* and therefore knowledge.

Simultaneous-existence-bodies are the woof and warp of Soul's loom. We can weave one whenever our heart desires. All bodies, realms, brotherhoods and *feelings*, are the interconnecting components of our true Self as we fulfill our inevitable evolutionary destiny.

Part IV

STAGES OF GROWTH

Chapter 19

STAGES OF THE FLOWER

Within the seed lies the bloom. Such are the stages of BEing that define ASCENSION:

The Dream Stage is the **Seed.**

The Lucid Stage is the **Sprout.**

The Purification Stage is the **Growth.**

The Transmutation Stage is the **Bud.**

The ASCENSION Stage is the **Bloom.**

First, we dream. This is called the Seed Stage. A seed is a powerful source of energy. For not only does the body rejoice in its consumption but the Spirit gladdens in its light. We recognize the dream experience as being an aspect of ourself that has become illuminated. Next, we become solidly and totally aware that we dream. This is called the Sprouting Stage. (Often in current literature on dream research, this is called lucid dreaming.)

Third, we begin to purify the mind and body through balanced thought, nutrition and elimination of body poisons. This is called the Purification Stage and

Diagram 3
THE FIVE STAGES OF ASCENSION

Five Stages of

Ascension

Seed

Sprout

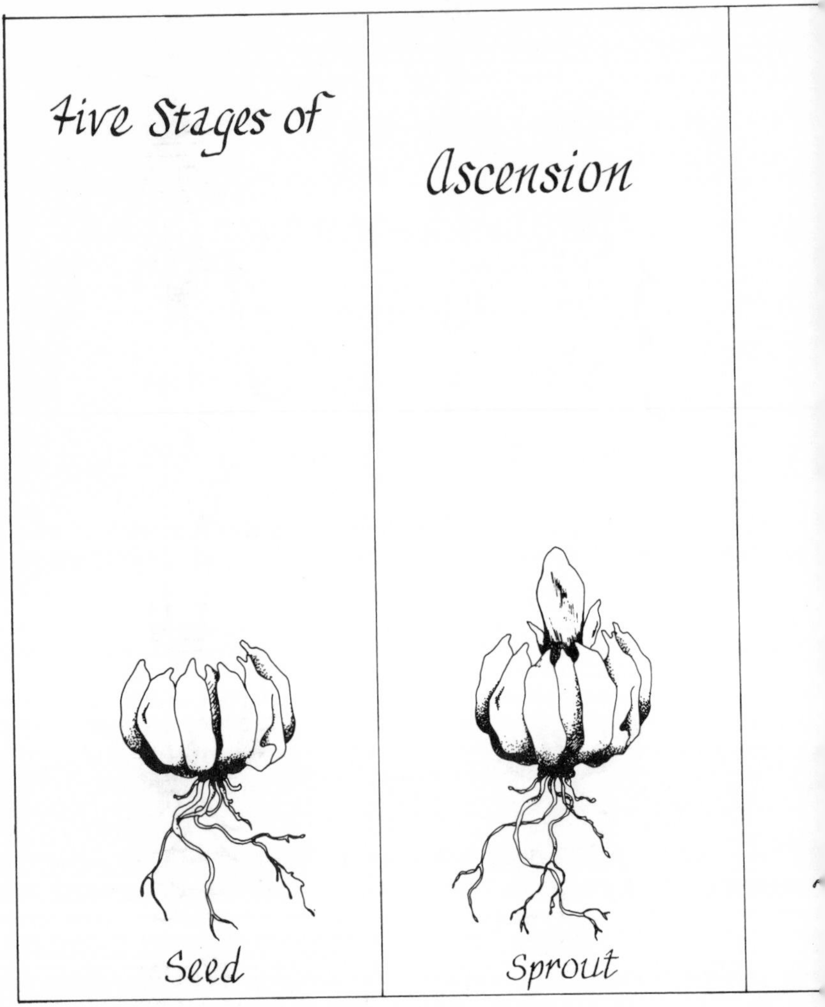

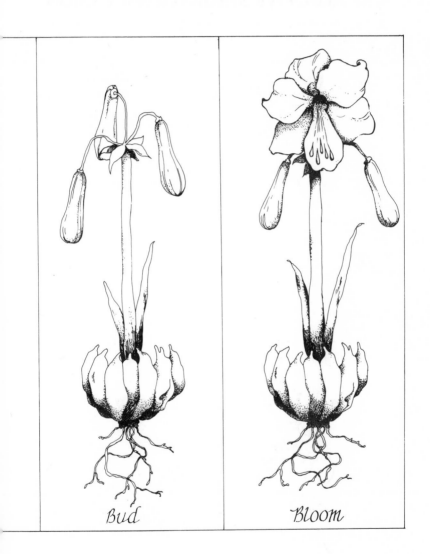

Bud   Bloom

relates to the growing stage of the plant.

Fourth is the Transmutation. This is called the Budding Stage. It is the beginning of the ability to change our vibrational body frequency to such a point that we would disappear on this realm or in the sight of others in this realm. We might visit other parts of our house, our planet, or any realm we choose.

Fifth is the ASCENSION. This is called the Blooming Stage. Total purity is attained within all body thoughts and cells at this point. We become the ASCENDED ONE. Our understanding of God and LOVE is then complete *feeling*. That *feeling* is the One Great Law of God — LOVE.

Chapter 20

STAGE I — THE SEED: DREAMS

A dream is an experience that is absolutely real in other realms.

To some of us this is a relief to know. We always suspected it although society has pegged dreams as everything *but* reality. Some reading this may even sense their ego's standing up in a defensive way because they have a great deal of *feeling* linked to their intellectual understanding of what dreams and dream symbology mean.

If we accept the premise that dreams are completely real in another realm, then we must do away, at least in part, with the word "dream" itself. Dream is a term which limits our spiritual BEingness by placing this all-important event into the category of illusion and fantasy. Thus the word dream is a misnomer. Henceforth I shall call these nightly experiences as true "seed stage" realities.

The confusion in understanding what a seed stage is goes back to the very roots of our social structure. In the past, tremendous fear was promulgated by feudal lords and priests to hold the masses in control. Guilt was introduced to man as a way for the ego to gain the upper hand. Through the priest-kings this manifested as vanity. Through the enthralled masses this was manifested as unworthiness. In this time few broke their egoic yokes to aspire to the ASCENSION. Those who did were either called witches or heretics and were destroyed and forgotten. In some cases, the Church cannonized them and made them Saints.

All the while, the undercurrent carried into this age. Men and women continued to spread their wings and look lovingly into their own lives at night (seed stage) seeking to understand their purpose here. The seed stage experience provided them with the escape for which they longed. It was a relief from the endless toil as a slave or the many senseless battles that ravaged their bodies, homes and families in the name of one cause or another.

Dreams are more than escape mechanisms. They are often considered as some surrealistic nonsense that is contrived because we ate too many plates of spaghetti or as symbols stored in our subconscious. This is far from the truth. As mentioned earlier, many understand their dreams as highly significant and are breaking their slavish ties to the past.

When scrutinizing the seed stage let us always remember that we are analyzing a reality — *not* a fantasy. Let us realize that analyzing the reality of the seed stage is no different than analyzing the reality of washing dishes on this planet.

Consider the Self as a multi-faceted being. Pry away from the *feeling* of separateness from God. Know that we have tendrils into all realms and places we wish to be. Then stretch the mind to realize that we create other "selves" at night and even in catnaps. The other "me" experiences a bit of knowledge and adventure in the realms, then that body dissolves upon awakening. This has already been described as a simultaneous-exist-ence-body.

The following is an example of a possible seed stage scenario, to show the place of symbology and the way it would be interpreted from that school of thought:

"You are in a restaurant eating. Someone calls your name. You go to the door and open it. A great river lies between you and your caller who is your mate, lover or family member on the other side. They are in distress and you want to reach them but there is no way. You frantically locate a rowboat and strive to cross. The current is strong and you sink into the water."

Then you wake in a confused, frustrated state. What does all this mean? You do not own a rowboat, have never seen the restaurant, and don't live near a great river.

First, look at the above seed stage from the view-point of many modern symbolical approaches to dream interpretation. The restaurant is a symbol of your state of consciousness at the moment, as would be any house or building in which you might find yourself. Since it was an eating place, it also represented a place and time of nourishment for your inner Self. If you are male and the

95

one who called you is female, this means that the feminine aspect of yourself (an anima figure) is making contact. If you are a female and the one who called you is a male, this means that the masculine aspect of yourself (an animus figure) is contacting you. The great river represents your own subconscious — the great unknown within you beneath the surface. The rowboat signifies your ability to provide a vehicle of transportation. It equates to the way you choose in waking life to get from point A to point B. The rapid current of the river indicates the great undercurrents running within your own subconscious self. These are so powerful as to divert you from your goal of reaching the other side and helping the masculine/feminine part of yourself to integrate in order to bring some understanding about a previous unaware desire into conscious life.

So there is imbalance in your ability to realize some aspect of your whole self and you fall into the river. The need to reach the other side wanes as now a great priority emerges — the need to survive. Now, you, the dreamer, are putting total energy into surviving the downward pull of your unknown fears (ego).

Another methodology of interpretation regarding dreaming would look at this same scenario from the *feeling* aspect. This is perhaps more valid and useful but not complete. For instance, the seed stage experience would be interpreted thus: "Mr. So-and-So, this dream left you *feeling* frustrated, angry, desperate and incomplete. When have you *felt* this way before? With whom?" In other words, it doesn't matter that you understand all the language of symbology but only that you get in touch with the *feelings* this experience brought you.

There is yet another discipline that examines dreaming from the standpoint of actual conversations occuring between authority/submissive figures — called topdog/underdog. It considers what you are asserting (topdog) or getting around (underdog). An example would be: You are the authority figure who is striving to reach the other shore. You are dominant and would attempt control of the mate you are rescuing. You would say, "You should know better than to be here or in trouble. You ought to do this or that, etc."

The underdog part of you on the other shore would say to the authority figure, "Yes, I'm sorry. I'm a worthless troublemaker." Yet all the time the underdog figure would be scheming a different way to slip around the topdog's authority and thus gain more reprimanding from the topdog, which in turn, reinforces the underdog who attempts again to display an even more subtle unworthy attitude. From this we see a fine example of the cruel interplay that the ego perpetuates upon the body.

Dream analysts have noted a curious thing. All people no matter where they live or what they do will have commonalities in their seed stage experiences. C. G. Jung called these "archetypes" and wrote at length on this subject. An example of an archetype is seeing or being in water in a seed stage experience. Water represents the *feeling* element that is underneath the surface of our subjective self. This archetype has the same meaning for all people in all countries.

Now let us take this same seed stage and look at it from the viewpoint of being real. You projected into another area or realm where some or all of these things: restaurant; river; rowboat; already existed or were created by you. (You can create instantly with a thought in the other realms). So your deepest, most intense *feelings* pictured themselves as actual palpable objects. The experience gave you the *feelings* you needed to deal with unfinished aspects of a relationship, which were real. Therefore, what you *felt* was real, and what you *did* was real, and helped resolve your old misunderstanding with the other person just as **solidly and realistically** as you would have in this realm.

How much interpretation does reality need? It needs acceptance. . . acceptance that all is happening in Divine Order and under the careful direction of those in the other realms who LOVE us. The sooner we realize that every thought and emotional desire is a kingly reality, the sooner we realize all that happens to us in daily waking life or nightly seed stage life is without exception the result of our own doing.

Indeed, it is our quest for LOVE that causes us to create disturbances in our nightly excursions. Because of LOVE we are allowed to create these "nightmares" of reality. It is the Soul striving to unveil itself from the ego.

The ability to create in the fourth realm (Earth) as well as any other realm is a gift of God. It goes on for one reason and one reason only. That is to reintegrate the separated ego energies back into ourself for the AS-CENSION. When we understand and *feel* all frustration, anger, guilt, shame, etc., belong to God and exist because of a lack of comprehension of the One Great Law, we will have ASCENSION in the palm of our hand.

The seed stage is our common denominator with each and every realm and all individuals therein. It is the first link to the other stages of growth in our inevitable evolutionary destiny.

Chapter 21

STAGE II - THE SPROUT : LUCID EXPERIENCES

In the spring when a seed stirs from slumber and lifts its gentle head toward the light of the sun, a dynamic occurrence begins. In the sleeping stage a seed is acid in chemical nature. When the seed sprouts it is no longer the acid sleeper, drowsy and dim in its understanding of who it is. It now has an identity, an awareness of heat, light, and the joy of nourishment and greenness. It now is alkaline in chemical nature. This is a radical change in plant consciousness.

To describe the lucid stage to someone who has never experienced it is like describing what it *feels* like to change the chemical nature of a safely shelled acid seed into a soft alkaline sprout. It is as tricky as being in the secure underground of ego and suddenly finding one's self thrust above the surface, staring into the blazing sunlit face of the One Great Law – LOVE.

For years I have listened to people talk of the singular experience in which they were solidly and lucidly somewhere else besides their bedroom on planet Earth. They might have denied its ever having happened except for the fact that it was so real. What *did* happen? Can it happen to anyone? Is it a reality? What exactly *is* the lucid stage of awareness?

It is the moment we become aware that we are in

the seed stage experience (dreaming) and suddenly realize we are aware and in control — "awake" within the dream.

The sprouting stage is our ability to say, "Hey, I am obviously *not* in my bed or on my couch on Earth. I am somewhere else. I *feel* myself breathing, I can touch and *feel* this wall and chair; I'm really here!" (Wherever 'here' is.) At that moment we have entered the sprouting stage of the journey to ASCENSION.

What is the purpose of becoming lucid? *Feeling* is the memory of the Soul. And there is no greater single experiential state that I know of than the lucid state for producing intense *feeling*. The more the Soul memory is activated, the more illumination is *felt* within the physical body. Conversely, the more we physically *feel* the more we activate the Soul. The lucid state is the strongest method we have for the accrual of Soul memory or *feeling*. Therefore this stage is *extremely important* in the process of changing the body to light.

Since we have established that the word dream is a misnomer, we must now view the term 'lucid dream' differently. We are aware. So we are 'lucid' and not dreaming.

INCONGRUOUS SITUATIONS

One helpful technique for realizing lucidity is to learn to look for incongruous situations while in the seed stage. Let's say we find ourself walking down a street close to home. It is very pretty. The trees are blossoming and scents are in the air. It is very uplifting and mellow. We suddenly come upon a rhinoceros head mounted to a tree upside down. The tree is solid purple and has eyeballs sticking out of it. At first, this jars us a bit because we have never seen anything like this before. When we regain our wits we realize that nothing of this nature could possibly exist in such a beautiful place. We decide we must be 'dreaming' (seed stage).

Having made this decision, we are at a critical point. We are on the threshold of understanding that we might be able to control some aspect of the events that are occurring. We are so close to realizing that we are lucid and solid in another dimension that we call this stage, 'pre-lucid.' We might say we are about to sprout. Spring is just starting to pull our head through the soil.

This fine line between being aware of another dimension as solid, and being as consciously in control as we are here in the fourth realm, is a crucial time. Our ego will be pulling so hard and so subtly that we are likely either to awaken or lapse back into the subjective state of the seed stage and continue our walk down the road, thinking purple-eyed trees and upside-down rhinoceros heads on our home street are altogether normal. This is when it is important to have done some prior homework such as selecting a key word or phrase before sleep in order to program ourselves that we are going to become lucid.

KEY WORDS

Pick any word or phrase, yet don't be concerned if this same word doesn't emerge in the seed stage. Just the fact that a word has been programmed into the mind before sleep will eventually yield results. For instance, the one that always appears for me is 'lucid.'

Examples of key words and phrases that others have programmed are: A good friend uses "hello." A young girl, "wow!" Another lady simply says, "I'm dreaming." There is no end to what our consciousness might pick.

Be sure to program in something like, "I'm going into the sprouting (lucid) stage tonight from the seed stage. The word or phrase I choose to help me is _____. Dear God, guide me in thy light." When we no longer believe that "this is only a dream (fantasy, imagination); it is not real," etc. then the key word is not as necessary.

Another technique is to program into the mind certain key words that will help to spot incongruent situations which lead us into the lucid (sprouting) stage. We can further ask that incongruent situations be manifested so that we *can* become 'pre-lucid' and spot these (such as the purple-eyed tree).

We are not only creating a fine line, but attempting to cross it when we use these techniques to enter the lucid experience. Do not get discouraged. Simply practice, practice and keep practicing, night after night. Do not relent.

104

ARM-DROP

This next technique called Arm-Drop is very useful.

Start your afternoon nap or nightly rest on your back. As you begin to relax, raise your arm, bending at the elbow so that the elbow is still on the bed or couch. As you drift further into light sleep, images usually appear such as a rock, the side of a building, a person standing nearby or something that you have previously dismissed as trivial and part of the misnomer 'dreaming.' These pieces of what you may have assumed to be fragmented fantasy or unconscious frustrations are nothing of the sort. They are objects in other dimensions. They exist in *actual places.* You might think, "These images flit so quickly, I am not grabbing onto them." If you go to see a movie and a picture of the Brooklyn Bridge flashes quickly on the screen, unless you have some personal association with it, you probably won't react emotionally or think about it very much. The fact remains, however, that you did see it. And more rapid than this glimpse of the Brooklyn Bridge movie is the ability of Soul to project instantly to any place it desires. The Soul simply views whatever it wishes at an amazingly accelerated speed.

As you enter into these beginning projections of other worlds your arm will drop. At first this will be startling and bring you out of the brief reverie on another dimension. After practicing several times nightly, you will begin to tie the *feeling* of the arm's falling to the bed, with becoming aware that *you are truly in another dimension*. Finally you will be able to have the arm fall gently instead of heavily and make the transition in consciousness to the place in which you are looking.

Actually you do this type of projection so many times in a day that you don't consider it to be anything but imagination. What a clever ego trap. *There is no imagination!* It is always an instantaneous projection of the Soul into another area. Once there, you can create as you wish because time, space, and matter are easily malleable in these vibrationally less dense areas. But with this freedom of creation comes responsibility. Just as you can make problems for yourself in this realm if you abuse or interfere with others, so it is possible in another dimension. Create all things in the name of LOVE, then you will not harm yourself or others.

Stabilize the moment you become aware you are somewhere else. Use the key word, repeating it many times if necessary and touch whatever objects can be found until they are actually *felt*. This stabilizes you further, along with use of the key word, into your self-made body which is usually a simultaneous existence. This temporary body allows you to fully experience some other realm of consciousness while maintaining your fourth realm Earth consciousness. You can question whoever you meet there to find out where you are and who they are. Again, one of the most important things to remember is that once you are viewing any images, know these are *real places.*

SEED STAGE JOURNAL

Another technique particularly useful is keeping a journal of seed stage sojourns. It will help you remember your interdimensional travels. You can also use a tape recorder and put it beside the bed to mumble into as you awaken in the middle of the night or early morning. Personally, I find this a superior method for recording my seed stage experiences in other realms.

The seed stage journal will help you get in touch with your creative ability on the other realms as well. When you view your carefully recorded seed stage experiences as complete reality long enough, you will step over the threshold with your 'key word' into the sprouting stage. I have watched this happen many times. You must be persistent.

To induce the lucid stage you can also review your journal of seed stage nightly experiences the next day. Then rewrite them, pretending you became lucid at some point and gained control of the situation. I have seen the value of this again and again. For quite often these experiences will repeat themselves and if you have remade the situation on paper or tape, the next time you reach that part of the experience in the seed stage you will remember what you wrote and become 'lucid.' This keys the consciousness that you are in another realm.

PRETEND LUCIDITY

Yet another way to help gain this stage is to pretend that your waking, daytime working situations are really seed stage experiences. Always look for a way to become more 'lucid' during an ordinary day. Repeat your key word or phrase. Question yourself, "Am I lucid?" Pay attention to the way things *feel* around you. Touch these objects and tell yourself that you are going to do this in your 'nightly reality' too. In other words, treat your waking days as the seed stage portions of your life. In experimenting with this technique I have had many fascinating realizations about how I related to daily life and how I took it for granted. This is one proven method that can catapult you into the wondrous lucid sprouting stage.

LOOKING AT HANDS

An old and interesting technique for gaining lucidity is looking at your hands. This involves programming yourself *before* you sleep so that in the seed stage you will remember to look at the back of your hands. When you do this, you will become aware that you are operating a different body on a different world other than this one. This is a highly effective method of becoming conscious of the sprouting stage.

STABILIZING

A tricky part of the lucid stage is when you succeed in realizing you are somewhere else but have trouble stabilizing your vision. This is a delicate time.

Let us say you have just become aware while in the seed stage and have looked down and seen your hands. You now know that you are somewhere else but all else is blurry. If you take your hand and beat it either against the ground or a convenient wall while saying your key word, you will begin to *feel* something. The wall will start to *feel* solid. Your hand will start to *feel* solid and the landscape will stop being fuzzy or spinning. In this same mode, if you don't remember to beat your hand into solidity then try placing your attention on a fixed point on the swirling or blurry landscape and hold that point until the landscape starts to clear and stabilize.

Have you ever been awakened suddenly from a deep sleep and for just a second or two seen everything as fuzzy and incoherent? The same thing happens when you move from the seed stage to the lucid sprouting stage. You are literally waking up again, but this time to a different reality.

MEDITATION ENHANCEMENT

A method I like to enhance lucidity is to sit quietly in a very comfortable chair. (I do this at the same time each day). The times recommended are early in the morning after a night's sleep and in the evening before retiring. While sitting there I start with a small prayer, asking God for assistance, and voicing what I will accomplish. Notice I said "will accomplish," for God holds us back from nothing; only we hold ourselves back. In the morning and at night I sit for about half an hour. If things begin to happen, I allow the time to go as long as needed. And what happens? First I allow the ego to play with thoughts of its own concerning the day, week, etc. After a short time, these play out. An example of this is having a fight with my boss that really didn't happen and as a result becoming emotionally embroiled.

It sometimes helps to use a word and chant it like a mantrum over and over to draw attention away from daily thoughts. I pick all manner of words like God, Christ, Aum, LOVE, or if I want to visit someone or some place in particular, I chant that name. I rarely chant it out loud for more than 20 seconds but continue to do this silently for several minutes. If I tire I simply stop. Do not force anything.

Usually after the daily squabbling thoughts have subsided I will see at least one image, maybe more. They will come quickly at first. Sounds of all types may accompany these images. If I am tired when I sit down to do a prayer, an image or color will pop up in front of me. The length of time required to make contact with an image will vary according to individual receptivity levels.

A helpful procedure is to pick an image such as a tree that appears most frequently in your seed stage experiences. You would know this reoccurring image through your journal of nightly experiences. After identifying this tree, make an affirmed statement before sleep that whenever you next see it you will become totally lucid at that moment. This will further impress the image of the tree into your nightly seed stage experiences triggering the necessary changes to become lucid.

Many times after the first prayer or meditation in the morning, plan an extra 45 minutes or so to go back to sleep. Often this is the best time of all to become lucid because you are relaxed and images of other realms flow easier and clearer. I use this quiet period to program in what I wish to achieve so that when I return to sleep it is easier for this experience to occur. This enables a rapid transition into another space.

When you do find yourself consciously on another realm, the energies can be intense and you may find it hard not to dematerialize and reawaken in your bed. In the beginning of your adventures, this could happen often.

THINK AND FEEL

Here is a method I like that further stabilizes me once lucidity is attained. I call it "Think & Feel." I say to myself, "I am *feeling* this place. I am *thinking* in this place. I am *feeling* this place," etc. . . . What this does is set up a link in the brain in which information and *feeling* flows between the cortex and the thalamus. This keeps me from becoming too excited or emotional while there.

111

On occasion there is tiredness in the body upon return from another dimension. Don't be confused or concerned about this. What has happened is that the body is flooded with new energies, ideas, and input when returning from another dimension. These energies are threatening to your ego. In other words, to exist in another realm, even briefly, is an impossibility to the ego and it will immediately begin discounting the experience. When you are lucid, however, the great energies generated are enough to reabsorb a portion of the ego's field. You are in essence reclaiming your own energy. A lucid experience makes your true Self stronger and your little self weaker.

The fatigue experience could be the result of the great amount of energy it takes to maintain a simultaneous-existence-body or work through an Oversoul. Where does the energy come from to do so? It appears to be a combination of universal, physical, and egoic energies. Not that you will always be tired... sometimes you feel just the opposite. You are refreshed and greatly uplifted. The only cause for being tired at all is the large amount of energy influx which burns off ego-toxins so rapidly that the physical body doesn't have a chance to eliminate the poisons quickly enough. When you have a lucid experience, poisons are loosened in the fourth realm body and must be detoxified through regular physical channels.

So do not be concerned. Take a hot shower and in no time at all, things will be normal again. That is, if after

112

you have been solidly in another world you can ever be normal by society's standards again!

A large number of people *are* now doing this lucid sprouting. About one third of the population on this planet has had at least one lucid experience. The number will be increasing in the days to come, for the energy aimed at our small globe from the other realms is immense.

EXPERIENCES IN THE LUCID STATE

I was contacted by an ASCENDED ONE and asked to include this section. So, lovingly here it is.

It is with reservation that I relate to you some of my own experiences, because I do not want you to look for these exact events to happen to you. Your path will form differently. Our similarities touch in the fact that you can manifest a simultaneous-existence-body that *feels* just as solid as you are now. I have had several hundred of these out-of-body experiences as they are commonly called.

1)   I materialized a lucid body on a turf of green grass. Above me were great spaceships of varied sizes, shapes, and colors. I was so amazed that I forgot to stabilize the body and within seconds lost this focus and returned to Earth.

Who knows where this experience might have led if I had stabilized myself and not been overcome by the phenomenon of the place?

113

There will be times when you will only be able to hold this lucid body for a few seconds. Don't be discouraged by this. Many different factors play into this such as your state of health on that particular night, the alignment of your goals with the Divine, etc. Keep practicing. Each night offers a fresh new opportunity. I have had scores of these very brief excursions. I consider each to be a triumph. So do not judge these as lost.

The lesson here was that I allowed the differences of this place to startle and imbalance me. When arriving at fascinating locales, immediately start chanting your key word over and over until you feel comfortable with the body you have manifested there. The influx of too much new data too quickly creates a shock effect and the large imbalance of energy hurtles you back into this realm.

2) I became partially cognizant of being somewhere else while looking at a man talking to me. I began chanting my key word, "lucid," over and over while touching objects to gain more focus. As soon as this body was intact, I listened to this man speaking. As it turned out, he was a friend of mine whom I know quite well.

   I immediately interrupted him and told him I was interdimensionally traveling and aware. I asked him to help me by making a superhuman effort to remember this so that when I awoke in Earth time, I could call him and confirm our meeting. He wholeheartedly accepted and I turned my attention to obtaining an object to bring back with me. This would prove beyond a shadow of a doubt that I had been somewhere else. We were in a dime store of some sort. I saw a child's toy that I liked but discovered I had no money. It was a little, purple, rubber lizard. I put this in my pocket after my friend paid ten cents for it. I then remembered that I slept with no clothes on, so that when I awoke on Earth, I would have no pockets. I took the toy out and tightly clutched it in my right hand. Saying good-bye to my friend, I dematerialized that body and awoke in my bed. My right hand was still tightly clutched and I *felt* the toy in it. I rejoiced then looked down at my opened hand for the toy. Nothing was there. I was bitterly disappointed. I called my friend immediately, even though it was early in the morning. He simply grunted, "No, I don't remember our meeting," and hung up.

The lesson in this was that although objects can be brought back from other realms, it is highly unlikely that we would see them since they are vibrating at a different frequency. Getting someone to remember on this level what an aspect of himself was doing on another level is quite uncommon although it happens. When it does happen usually it will appear to the other person like a seed stage experience (dream).

3) There are times when you will become lucid and wonder if you weigh a thousand pounds because it is very difficult to arise from the chair in which you

find yourself. The following is such an account:

I materialized in what looked like my own bedroom sitting in the same chair that I have used for these journeys over a thirty year period. Upon attempting to get up, I found I could not. My legs simply would not move. Finally with great determination, I stood, breathed deeply and moved. I walked downstairs noting carefully all the differences in this house and my own back on Earth. I was overjoyed at finding the grass really red just as I had always thought. The body dissolved after that. Whether this is actually true or not, it is what appeared before my lucid eyes and at that moment was just as real to me as the couch you are sitting on is to you.

This experience yielded two important points. First, even though the body may feel hopelessly heavy in some of our lucid awakenings, we *can* move. Keeping our attention on this can make it happen. Second, we assemble our own worlds and *can* shape them in thousands of different ways and colors. This is the power of God. And we are God.

The reason that objects sometimes seem so familiar in these places is because we are using the memory of another Oversoul counterpart and to them it is very familiar, like our living room. Only because we are aware of being in two places at the same time will any differences be noticed. For instance, the door will be in a different place, the fireplace and stove will look different, etc. But to the body we have manifested, these changes will appear normal.

4) I awakened in front of a small motel. From a distance I could see other people. I was already stabilized. Not being particularly pleased with where I was, I decided to project into another realm. As I attempted running and jumping I could get nowhere. My feet barely left the ground. Suddenly, I remembered a technique which a friend of mine had told me. He said to let yourself fall forward and you would begin to float, then fly. So I did this. Instead of floating or lightening up, I hit the ground with great momentum. As I lay there, nose in the gravel, I began to feel a familiar sensation — pain. Pain is a reality even in the other realms. These bodies we create are able to see, smell, taste and especially — *feel.* I heard other people running over to me and asking if I was all right. I *felt* very embarrassed and got up and walked off. Despite the pain, I decided this was obviously where I was supposed to be and sat on the gravel looking out across a rather pleasant view of distant hills. I took time to observe the differences in that realm and the clothes I was wearing. The body dissolved as I was examining the strange currency in my pockets.

I learned from this to stick with techniques that work for me!

Numerous times I have become lucid inside a

117

house or building of some sort and realizing I had a very limited time in that area, sought a way through the structure by forceful projection through walls. In most cases I would lose my focus and the body would dissolve. I have learned to find a door and walk outside. Going through walls and ceilings takes a tremendous amount of energy. This *feeling energy* could be used to carry us into another state of awareness where incredible experiences await. Use the door.

It is important to know that wherever you find yourself upon lucid awakening can be changed. This is a function of Free Will. Why do you decide to go for a walk one hour and a movie the next? This is because of your Free Will, because it pleases you to do so.

Frequently, I materialize a form in a room or locale that is not very interesting. Occasionally it is nighttime there. To alter this and make something useful occur, I decide to do something different. It works exactly the same way here in this realm as it does in some of the other realms. To get somewhere interesting we have to get off our buttocks and go do it.

5) I found myself at the home of a rather large family and established solidity by controlled breathing and touching myself. However, I decided to enter another dimension that I *felt* might be more interesting. I proceeded to sit down in a chair and meditate in order to leave, when the mother of that family came and asked me to join them for dinner before I could focus. They were so nice that I

agreed.

We sat at a long rectangular table. Every age was represented from young to old. The food was delicious. Suddenly I felt ill at ease because I might not have much time left in this simultaneous existence. I started chanting aloud in order to leave that area and climb higher. The entire family stopped and stared at me with intense blue eyes and began to chant this same word with me. I stopped chanting and stared as they began to increase their pitch of chanting, still in unison. Only then did I realize I was in the presence of a group of very advanced Souls. I was so startled I could no longer hold lucidity and began to fade, returning to my bed. I had been fed and nurtured by the Souls I sought without knowing it, but hadn't had the awareness to recognize it until the final moment.

In conclusion, don't be concerned about leaving where you are if it doesn't interest you. You are the one that makes life interesting. God gives you the opportunity but doesn't run your life. Live life as it seems best to you, here and in the other realms.

6) We will see and feel many unique cultures and spacecrafts from time to time. We may even change our own form dramatically. The body manifested may be much older or younger or even a different color. The following is an example:

I awoke in a crib in a nursery. I saw my arms

and legs flailing in the air. I was about 6 months old. To have the awareness I do now and to be trapped in that tiny helpless body was quite unsettling. I *felt* the emanations of other children's thoughts. They were like tidal waves of emotion sweeping over my defenseless form. When an adult came in, I thought I would perish because of the dissident vibrations coming from her. Yet she was the one assigned to attend me. Finally the energies of this body waned and I utilized this opportunity to project elsewhere. I found myself as an adult again swept up in a great wind and carried through a giant window by an unseen force into another dimension. My body changed for the third time and I tumbled into a great ball of light, and felt joy beyond words. I could not hold onto this place and awakened in my bed on Earth once again.

From this I gained a healthy respect for the experiences children go through.

7) I stabilized a body in a large yard during a family picnic. Although I recognized none of the people, they seemed to know me quite well. I decided to leave this place as nothing significant was happening. I began to levitate myself and as I did, a teenage girl came up to me and asked if she could go with me. She called me "uncle." As soon as the others saw what was happening they all wanted to go. I said a prayer aloud and began levitating all of them. As

I did so, I *felt* a gigantic spiral of joyous *feeling* rotate in my midsection and quickly consume me. With this much power, I easily levitated everyone. The *feeling* of joy was so intense that I lost the form there.

This particular experience taught me that when I serve others by helping them to elevate their *feelings*, I empower myself.

Often *feelings* gained in the lucid adventure will return with us into this realm. This is very important. Truly, it is one of the main reasons for even attempting the lucid state. And we will continue to *feel* in every form until we decide that joyousness is the best way to BE. For it is through great and joyous *feeling* that we AS-CEND.

A question often asked is, "I had this incredibly real experience... was I lucid?" My answer is invariably the same. If you have to ask, you were *not* lucid. There is no more doubt about being lucid than there is whether you are alive and consciously reading this sentence.

Chapter 22

STAGE III - THE GROWTH: PURIFICATION

Definition of the
Pythagorean Master Number 22

THE MASTER BUILDER

The Essence of Divine Spirit gathers. By living truth in his physical existence, he bridges Heaven and Earth. The Light Bearer touches the hand of the Immortals.

If we can envision what it is to be totally and systematically cleansed in body, thought, speech, and emotions, then we have glimpsed the intent of the growing stage - The Purification.

The earth particles drop off our sprouting stage head and the newness of green birth gives way to a firm stalk-purpose of mature understanding. The lure of ASCENSION thrusts us upward from the Earth. We are now in the midst of life and know what we want.

As we propel every aspect of BEingness toward the light of LOVE, the intensity of our growing stalk becomes increased in magnification. For only a strong, mature stalk of experienced wisdom can hold the delicate yet potent bloom whose rarefied petals light far more brilliant than the sun.

All life, and all Great Ones, humbly offer help. We are purifying the body and the universe is opening its arms to receive and assist in a good stout scrubbing. So great becomes the joy of our guides and Oversouls at this point that it can barely be contained. We choose LIFE. A more potent decision is impossible to make. Drawbridges of the mind and heart collapse in front of us awaiting our sacred march across their tender timbers. Nothing will hold us back. A fiery image of the ISness, the One LOVING God, lies exposed and riveted in hot stamped wax upon the seal of our hearts.

Though we may not totally *feel* the One Great Law, we are now the well-informed and insistent hound that sniffs at the heels of Transmutation and ASCENSION.

What exactly does 'being purified' mean? How do we know we need it? When are we purified enough? Being purified means to rise as a growing stalk and shed any unnecessary fibers and attitudes that would stand in the way of totally *feeling* LOVE.

Let us take an individual case. We will call him Elmo. He could be thought of as every-man, every-woman. Let us assume that Elmo has read the manual up to this point. He has mentally accepted the idea that he is God and LOVES himself. Mentally, he understands and agrees with the concept that there is no such thing as dreams. They are, instead, total realities occurring on another dimension that he, Elmo, is conscious of being able to control. Let us now project into the future and assume that Elmo has diligently practiced the techniques as outlined in the Lucid Sprouting Stage and has attained conscious, solid, *feeling* control in the Lucid Stage at least one time.

Elmo is obviously excited as he returns to his physical 4th realm body and knows that something very special has happened to him. How will it change him?

At first there is discouragement because what occurred in that one experience *felt* so good and was so uplifting; then suddenly he finds himself back in the same situation, i.e. having to go to work, pay bills, etc.

What happened to Elmo in that one experience was a part of the Purification. When Elmo returned to his body, a small portion of the ego reintegrated into his Soul energy pattern. He regained a piece of what he had lost earlier. He became a little wiser through the *feeling* of this experience and truly one step closer to understanding the One Great Law.

This is Purification. It is not a fixed stage but more of an awareness of *feelings*. It is confusing for some. They want an A-B-C approach to ASCENSION.

It could start simultaneously with reading this manual, as it did with Elmo. Anytime a hindering attitude is changed for the better, its energy is reintegrated for our total use. This affects the physical body and changes occur at a cellular level.

At the cellular level are tissue acid toxins. With an attitude change, these are released into the blood and lymph system for removal by our eliminative channels. Every attitude that would limit full expression of the One Great Law has a correlating toxic acid deposit somewhere in the physical body. Some of these trapped acid waste products are inherited. The rest come from a lack of choosing the correct foods and exercise.

Take Elmo for instance. He knows that refined "junk" foods are plugging him up and causing all sorts of lowered energy manifestations. How can he expect to ASCEND when he stuffs himself with greasy hamburgers surrounded by refined bread and fries? He knows now that proteins (meat) and starches (bread, fries) do not mix in the stomach. They produce putrification, poisoning, tissue congestion and death of cells. When he was younger neither he nor his parents knew about dietetics. He still, however, has an opportunity to clean himself inside out.

If a cell is congested and poisoned with acids it will not be capable of producing the bright, white light of incandescent beauty which is required for ASCENSION. Instead, seen clairvoyantly, the cell will appear dark red, brown or black.

One way to study the changes that occur during the Purification is through iridology. This is the study of the iris (colored portion) of the eye. It has been developed since the early 1800's and is extremely accurate. The iris contains thousands of nerve fibers. Within each of these fibers are tens of thousands of even smaller fibers which feed directly into the brain and are an accurate picture of what is happening physically, emotionally, and mentally.

As we detoxify and change destructive attitudes into constructive ones, the iris reflects a color change. I have seen brown eyes change to blue. This is very dramatic. It is suggested that someone well-versed and studied in the practice of iridology monitor the irises as these dynamic growth stage changes occur.

In this way the process of Purification can be better understood.

Chapter 23

PURIFYING THE FINER STATES
OF CONFUSION

Pertinent topics that could slow the Soul progress of a sincere seeker are presented here.

UNREALISTIC GOALS

Unrealistically difficult goals are a subtle trap. And with the idea of goal-making so lauded in this time by our educators, realistic and unrealistic personal expectations need differentiation.

Without realistic goals, buildings would not be started or finished and all of the material aspects of this world would lack vision and the expediency to manifest vision.

When we create goals that are outside our immediate experience of *feeling*, a predictable situation occurs in the body. We *tighten* around the heart center. This constricts the flow of energies coming into this area. This creates circulatory difficulties.

An architect would not do this. He or she would construct a plan that is difficult but still within their scope of conceivability through *feeling*. Experience tells them it is possible. The contractor may or may not accept the plan based on his knowledge of building and his personal understanding of his own abilities to do such projects. If the contractor accepts, usually it is because his *feelings* suggest to him that this architectural goal is achievable and feasible.

Thus, we have a goal that is meticulously charted out and methodically executed. In the business world, goals that come to fruition are usually handled in this manner.

Another set of goal-makers is being addressed here, however. They go to outlandish lengths to plot out maps of intricate spiritual ideals. **The fallacy is that these well-meaning persons base their goals on the feelings of others.**

I have listened to persons heavily stressed because they didn't *feel* they were making the same spiritual progress as their friends. They could not understand why they were not achieving their well-plotted goals. They blamed themselves and entered into a web of unworthiness.

Even this manual could create such an effect on its readers. They learn of ASCENSION and then become fearful that they will not achieve the goal. This is the sneaky ego manifesting again. Questions asked are, "Will I ASCEND in this lifetime? . . . What if I don't? . . . I want to finish everything *this* time around."

Not ASCENDING in this period does not mean failure. There is no failure. There is only the divine plan of GOD and HIS allowance of letting each of us explore all the nuances of its ever wondrous contents in our own ways and at our own speed.

Simply BE what and who we are by living each day

to our own personal best and appreciate the opportunities to do so. Toy with the concepts offered in this manual as a child plays with his building blocks. Create ways for this information to serve as a child makes a house out of pinestraw.

There is only one place to start with any form of spiritual understanding. That is right where we are in our *feelings on planet Earth* at this moment.

This manual is written in five stages for a reason. That is to let us know that there is a place we individually fit in as we *feel* toward our inevitable evolutionary destiny. Indeed, we will find elements of ourselves scattered through these five stages.

Looked at from the usual "I achieve" perspective of this planet, ASCENSION is a goal. Looked at from the viewpoint of the Brotherhoods, **ASCENSION is a feeling.**

Have goals. They are important. Consider whether or not they are realistic at the stage from which we *feel*. If they are, then we are already half-way to that goal. If they aren't, we might create a great deal of confusion and frustration.

The Soul has no goals. It already IS. God has no goals. It already IS too.

THE SEXUAL QUAGMIRE

What exactly happens to the energy patterns of each partner in a sexual relationship?

When engaging in sexual intercourse with another,

you take on that person's energy patterns and these energies circulate with your own for thirty days. This means that you not only carry your attitudes but also those of mate or partner. Assume your partner has had sexual relations with nine other partners in a thirty day period and then has intercourse with you. You will then have the emanations of ten individual energy patterns in your aura. All of the inharmonious attitudes of these persons will serve to weaken and eventually destroy the carrier of same if prolonged.

Further, let us assume that the nine other partners have had intercourse with nine other people, even if it be unknown to partner number one, then the sum total of all these discordant energies is floating around in the aura of the participant.

This information is not given as a basis of judging the Self or others. It is offered so that we may better discern those practices which could lead us away from the road of ASCENSION.

CELIBACY

Celibacy is not just physical abstinence, but a mental and emotional one too. If one wishes to be celibate, yet has thoughts and emotions that are of a sexual nature, he is not being completely celibate, and confusion reigns.

True celibacy is as natural a state as eating or sleeping. There should be no struggle involved in its practice. If there is, then at some level, joy is stifled, and again confusion is created.

Often we will *feel* the desire to be celibate for a period of time just to balance the sexual energies within ourselves. For the creative drive is indubitably a powerful force for the production of *feeling* in our bodies. When successfully turned inward, it could power the cells to spin faster, producing more *feeling* and light. However, celibacy has mistakenly become a rite of passage to ASCEND.

Let us delve further into this confusing topic.

When one becomes lovingly involved with one's mate and the sexual union occurs, great power is generated. The deep relaxation that happens after lovemaking further opens the heart for tremendous healing and revelation. This great power can be turned upward into the head.

There is the idea that a man who loses his semen is weakened. That argument has two sides, however. Since God is all things, then the release of our sexual fluids is not a loss. For how can we lose anything if God lives in our partner as well? Nevertheless, if a man and woman join their bodies with any purpose other than making love to God, they will lose strength at some level. Lovemaking is for the glorification of the divine in each of us. This sacred act is really a prayer to the Father. Why do you think God gave us the ability to *feel* this physical union? It is God we are LOVING. Considered thusly, lovemaking assumes the holy place it deserves and will not be a loss of strength but a substantial gain. It is only when thoughts of egoic desires dominate

133

lovemaking, that lust is produced clouding the mind and dissipating energy.

We gain or lose energies for ASCENSION through lovemaking if we choose to and *only* if we choose to. Ultimately, then, we *gain or lose* energies for ASCENSION through celibacy by our choice of thoughts.

So the issue of celibacy remains one of individual need. If one *feels* the need to be celibate, fine. God will support him. If one *feels* the need to have a loving partner, fine. However, if one *feels* that he *must* be a celibate just because of some teaching or some person before him ASCENDED by being thus, then this individual is slavishly deluded by another.

SOULMATES

The concept of Soulmates can be a definite stumbling block.

To begin with, no one has to be joined with another in any sort of relationship in order to transmute and ASCEND the body. This does not mean that spending our lives with a mate is not highly beneficial and satisfying. A relationship is a wonderful way of generating powerful *feelings* and *feelings* eventually turn the body to light. But we have these *feelings* individually; we ASCEND as individuals. And if we wait for a Soulmate, we may be waiting for a long time.

To become unified with anything, we must completely *feel* these three words—**God is One**. If we depend on another person or mate to ASCEND, we will be caught in another finer state of confusion.

UNCONDITIONAL LOVE

The term unconditional LOVE creates a subtle state of confusion. People speak about how unconditional LOVE must be expressed by loving others no matter what they do or say. Yet, these same people unknowingly condition LOVE by their prejudiced views and seem to revel in laying guilt on their own shoulders and those they misguide. Let us examine this vaguely defined and elusive ideal.

If we could LOVE our physical body as much as our body LOVES our thoughts, we would be LOVING unconditionally. The body LOVES our thoughts so much that it immediately molds itself according to whatever *feeling* and thought we pour upon it and does this without question, with total abandon, with mathematical precision.

To experience true unconditional LOVE merely stare at yourself in a mirror. Reflected there you will see an outstanding example of how much the body unconditionally LOVES your *feelings* and forms your physiology to match the shape of the body and level of health. **We live with unconditional LOVE every moment of our lives.** The difference between those who have AS-CENDED and those who have not is then made clear. The ASCENDED ONES consciously LOVE their thought with as much zeal and devotion as their bodies LOVE their thoughts. This interaction then alters the body chemistry to light and thus immortality is evidenced.

JUDGMENT OF EMOTIONS

Finally, one of the most destructive states of confusion is that of judgment of our emotions. This means all kinds of emotions including anger, hate, jealousy, fear, and apathy. We begin creating bodily destruction and mental confusion when we *judge* these *feelings* after having them.

Any *feeling* other than one that brings harmony or is harmonious to the physical body is a judgment. For example, if you are angry it is because something or someone was either right or wrong, good or bad. It is the result of *feeling* that your way is better than another's.

If a method or procedure you have developed is better than another's, that indicates that you *feel* a worse or inferior method exists by comparison. To be angry, you must *feel* that you are right and that you have been wronged. To be fearful, you must *feel* that bad or evil is happening and that good has fled. To be apathetic, you must *feel* worthless and that worthiness, which is good, has escaped you. To be unaware you must *feel* unworthy of knowing.

Discernment is the key. It is not that you are right, wrong, good, bad, evil, better, worse, worthy or unworthy. It is that you have a different view. The *truth* is a relative matter. Everyone of us is the truth. Hostility and dissident *feeling* eliminates itself by eventually destroying the physical bodies of those who harbor such *feelings*.

For instance, if we become angry about or at someone, we are really angry at ourselves. These emotions would not be so destructive to the body if afterward we didn't judge ourselves so harshly about being angry at the other person.

It is not anger itself, but judgment of ourselves for having anger that causes mental confusion. When we state that we are confused about something, then realize it is because we are judging ourselves for some emotional condition. It can even occur from an off-the-cuff remark about something or someone that we do not *feel* meets our particular set of values. **Even done lightly, judgment of any nature eventually leads to confusion.** God is not confused, because God does not judge ITself. Why should we?

It is as natural to have these emotions as it is to breathe. And it is as unnatural to judge these *feelings* as it is to suffocate. These strong *feelings* of anger, fear, and jealousy are stages of the One Great *Feeling* — LOVE. It is LOVE expressed with aspects of ego, but it is LOVE nevertheless. And to suppress it with self-judgment about having these *feelings* will destroy the body.

The formula for physical death is: Judgment = Confusion = Pain.

The formula for eternal life is: Feeling = Intuition = LOVE. There are no hidden integers or cryptic codes. There is only this simple magic equation. The *feelings* of joy, happiness, and enthusiasm evidence the absence of self-judgment.

It is the one who no longer acknowledges extremes that finally realizes the joy, enthusiasm, and energy of inner harmony. This can best be achieved in a heart free of the finer states of confusion. In conclusion, we must follow our *feelings*, for they are the most sacred texts we have.

Chapter 24

PURIFYING FUNCTIONS OF
NON-RESISTANCE

When we quit resisting anything and start LOVING, the One Great Law manifests a perfect situation for us. No one or no thing can resist LOVE. Jesus did not strike back when smote across the face. Nor did he resist being crucified. His perfect example of non-resistance changed the way of the world from that time to this. He taught and lived the One Great Law of LOVE and did not resist any aspect of lesser consciousness.

Therefore, he ASCENDED. And so can we.

The more we LOVE, the less resistance in the form of plaque will deposit itself along the walls of the arteries. Circulatory problems are the result of resistance to the allowance of increased *feeling*. The circulatory system is a barometer for this. Our very blood courses in accordance to how much we LOVE.

When any thought-*feeling* less than pure LOVE enters the heart center, some degree of circulation starts resisting the flow of its own precious fluids. Muscles tighten, enzymes stop being produced, minerals don't absorb, vitamins and food fail to be assimilated by the very cells of our wondrous temple. At that point we are choosing the path of death.

If we catch ourselves resisting something, we might

do the following: Pray to God that this object (person, thing, etc.) be surrounded in a bubble of pure white blazing Light. After this is done decide whether you *feel* the same about the situation. If so, then put this white bubble around yourself also. Now, turn the whole picture over to God and say something like this, "I do only Thy Will, not mine. I hold Thy LOVE within. I choose to not-resist the One Great Law that circulates freely even now in my heart." If a peaceful *feeling* does not come immediately after doing this affirmation, practice the bubble of light again then repeat the affirmation.

Whatever we resist, will haunt us, be it person, place or thing. It will lay siege to our BEingness as firmly as if we were to lasso it about the neck and drag it with us. Be certain then, if we resist anything we shall draw to us that thing which we resist.

For example, let's take our friend Elmo again. What he resists is an aspect of his job. It involves drilling holes into 4 lb. steel blocks and then loading them onto a platform. He despises this portion of his job. He *feels* anger in his heart about it. He *feels* like his factory engineer should create a machine to make his situation better. He views this part of his job as needless hard labor. By resisting what he has chosen and *feeling* that resistance in his heart, he draws to himself an extra stack of steel blocks to be handled the next night on his shift. He complains to his foreman and is told he can quit if he doesn't like it. So his resentment increases toward his work and his foreman. And as his *feeling* of resistance increases, more and more steel blocks seem to appear for him to cut on his shift. Suddenly he realizes it is *he* that is responsible for all resistances or blockages. So Elmo changes his *feelings* about the extra work load and begins to whistle happy tunes and bless every single steel block.

On the very next day he discovers his workload is back to normal and even decreases. His foreman comes around and says very nicely that he got the number of steel blocks greatly reduced. He even tells Elmo that he is doing his job so well that he recommended a pay raise.

To demonstrate the principal of Non-Resistance which is a part of the One Great Law, an example is taken from the works of Aikido, a Japanese martial art. It is called the "Unbending Arm."

First, have a friend stand and extend one arm in front of him, with the palm up. You hold one hand over his biceps muscle and the other under his forearm. Ask him to resist you as you bend his arm at the elbow by pushing down on the biceps muscle and up on the forearm. After you have bent his arm upward, have him to repeat this procedure with the following changes. Ask him to put his attention on a round point about one inch below his navel. Tell him to envision this point reducing by one-half its size not letting it disappear. While he is doing this and has his attention on this point, you attempt to bend his arm at the elbow as before. This may surprise you and him. The arm will not bend if the attention is totally on the one point, no matter how hard you push, yet he will not be making any effort whatsoever to resist you.

Holding one point below the navel in the mind's eye, greatly increases the release of a substance known as chyle throughout the system. Its great alkalizing force allows LOVE to flow unobstructed, rushing into and tremendously strengthening all the energy centers throughout the body. This exercise supports the major premise that: **when LOVE is truly flowing, we are in the most relaxed and strongest state possible.**

INTUITION

Intuition functions only when there is non-resistance. It is a knowingness based on a higher level of subtle *feeling*. Every day we experience this subtlety at least once but just brush it off and think nothing of it. In that moment of openness, our pineal gland is functioning as it should. It is instructing us via the Soul pertaining to some action in life.

The pineal gland is the seat of intuition and principal receiver of light through the eyes and into the major energy centers. However, when the body is toxic, light is blocked from the pineal and causes calcification. The numerous drugs fostered by the last few generations have also made the tissue of the pineal gland toxic.

Another factor of extreme import is blood flow into the pineal area. This is blocked mostly by a physiological stress factor that squeezes the tissue surrounding the arteries and veins going to and from the pineal, thereby greatly reducing necessary nutrients and oxygen.

When intuition is functioning, there is no stress to cause a blood flow restriction. Nor is there any ego blocking the flow of light into the pineal from the eyes. Therefore the light, which is energy, stimulates the pineal to produce the necessary hormones further triggering the hypothalamus and pituitary gland. The pituitary gland then activates the rest of the body with a certain *feeling—intuition*. We are left with the decision whether to pay attention to it or not. If we choose to acknowledge our intuitive leads, we are paving the way for more and more intuitive *feelings* to follow. This brings greater light and blood flow to feed, decalcify and detoxify the pineal gland.

Allow all intuitive *feelings* and do not let the ego denigrate them as silly or unimportant.

Envision the pineal gland glowing brilliantly while using this affirmation, or create a similar one:

> Great ONENESS! Flood me with thy blazing white flame of Transmutation and total LOVE. Remove all desires that hinder cleanliness and block ASCENSION. Transmute their causes and effects throughout all time. Replace this with Your Omnipresence and establish Ubiquitous Beingness within me forever!

Do this at least three times a day and visualize a white flame pouring from above the head to the feet and extending for several feet surrounding the body in a cylinder of light.

143

Hold the image, *feel* the flame permeating every molecule. If this be done and *felt* regularly, most, if not all, cellular poisons will be transmuted into powerful illuminating consciousness.

KUNDALINI

The Kundalini is the name given to a particular portion of purification when certain channels in the body are unblocked. As the stalk grows upward on the flowering plant so does Kundalini rise from the base of the spine to the crown of the head. This energy resembles a DNA molecule with its double helix structure. And what are blocks and toxins? — Ego manifestations.

The rapid spiralling up and down of this strong connecting force between the base of the spine to the head, signals that a fine point of integration has occurred between the Autonomic and Central Nervous System.

Kundalini can manifest as a searing heat that clears its final path up the spine and into the head or it can happen in stages which are not as dramatic as an all-at-once experience. Many minor steps occur, which can appear dramatic in themselves. Remember that all people experience differently.

In my case, I ran a high fever with no other symptoms for two weeks. In the second week of fever I had a seed stage experience in which I was naked, scrubbed by some women then pushed into a room with a large basket. A gigantic python came out of the bas-

144

ket and before I could run away, it bolted through the air and bit me on the leg. I screamed into consciousness in holy terror and *felt* electricity course through every cell of my body. I almost passed out from the electric *feeling* that lasted intensely for several seconds and persisted mildly for several hours. Coupled with a high fever and the inability to eat or drink anything except water, I thought I was done for.

Days later, I suffered from convulsions of a strange nature, and sought medical help. I was convinced I had malaria or some exotic illness. The tests all proved negative. I had nothing, or so I was told. A strong drug was prescribed to help with symptoms. Instead it made me much worse. I dragged myself to the toilet and flushed the drug.

The fever finally broke and within two days I was back at 100% function, as though nothing had occurred. This was the beginning of my Kundalini's rising. Impurities were simply being burned out of my body. Within three months of this experience I made my first contact with the Great White Brotherhood.

Over a period of weeks, while in prayer, I saw thousands of silver specks on different backgrounds of color. The Brotherhood informed me that they were my own life force being transmuted into available energy. The different fields of color were the different chakras that were being fine tuned.

Lastly, a great volcano blast went off in my head during one prayer period and I saw a dazzling white sky above me with sharp edges around the sides. It was as though I were in a volcanic cone looking upward at the sky right after the top of the mountain had blown off.

Understand that the Kundalini energy, which is a total integration of the two nervous systems, occurs when we are completely conscious and not in any altered state such as deep meditation. For integration means just that. We are totally conscious and *feel* this awakening when it is complete. Do not *feel* fearful of Kundalini or this will block it. Do not look forward to it as though it must happen or this will hamper it. Simply continue purifying in all ways.

Be assured that the experience of Kundalini does not need to be painful or distracting if proper purification and understanding has preceded the experience. It can be highly pleasurable and enlightening.

There are those that have had this experience in another life and were born with very strong genetic constitutions and clean bodies. For these persons, there need not be the heavy burn-off of poisons (ego) to reach that same *feeling* state.

However, this is not ASCENSION. It is a stage in the purification process.

Chapter 25

PURIFICATION OF THE CHAKRAS

Chakra is the Hindu name given for etheric energy centers that are located close to major nerve ganglions in the physical body. There are two sets of these — the major chakras and the subchakras.

Chakras are affected by the force of our emotions and translate these into physical responses. (See Diagram 4.)

At any chakric level *feeling* can become trapped. Ultimately, every single *feeling* travels upward through the chakras to the crown. All emotions are expressions of the One Great Law, we simply qualify them by transient *feelings*.

THE SEVEN MAJOR CHAKRAS

Consider the root chakra which is located at the base of the spine and is the area of unawareness. There *feelings* can be evidenced by statements such as "I don't know" or "I'm not creative." This perpetuates the *feelings* of unworth and attitudes of depression. For we are choosing to be unaware. In truth we know everything all of the time. What hurts the body and lessens our chances at Transmutation is not only that we just say, "I don't know." The damage occurs because we judge ourselves for not knowing. There is often a momentary *feeling*

Diagram 4
MAJOR CHAKRAS AND EMOTIONAL
AWARENESS SCALE

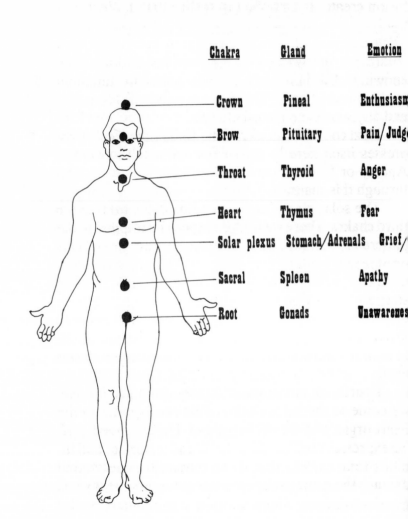

Chakra	Gland	Emotion
Crown	Pineal	Enthusiasm
Brow	Pituitary	Pain/Judg
Throat	Thyroid	Anger
Heart	Thymus	Fear
Solar plexus	Stomach/Adrenals	Grief/
Sacral	Spleen	Apathy
Root	Gonads	Unawareness

within of confusion and stupidity after stating this phrase. A way to avoid the destruction that this confusion creates is first of all to realize that it affects our bodies adversely. Instead, reword this phrase to state, "The ego part of me chooses not to know. The God within me always knows." When this is done "not knowing" is a choice, not a self-judgment or statement of ignorance. Physiologically the body will not suffer and all *feelings* are placed in a wholesome perspective.

Next consider the sacral chakra. Trapped *feeling* expresses itself here in the spleen and small intestines. Apathy or "I don't care *feelings*," are communicated through this chakra.

The solar plexus nerve ganglion is the area of the third chakra. There we find *feeling* can be trapped in the pancreas, adrenal glands, stomach and liver. This entrapment leads to the expression of grief, sometimes deep and certainly damaging. Statements such as "I feel so sad, or I can't go on," are stimulated by ego here. It disperses the atomic electron structure which could end in death. I have often observed this pattern of vibrational atomic electron dissipation in those affected at this level.

Fourth, on our upward journey toward full *feeling* we come to the heart chakra. This corresponds to the heart organ and the thymus gland. Here trapped *feeling* expresses itself as "fear," and it so terrorizes and inhibits total LOVE, that it can physically squeeze and damage the heart itself. Fear directly alters the thymus gland which is the fountainhead of our immune system

149

adversely affecting the entire cellular level.

A way to prevent fear from harming the body is to prioritize our wording regarding it. For instance, say, "What I am *feeling* is the emotion of fear. It is harmless to the body as long as I don't judge myself or others for having it. I allow it to pass through me. I allow it to stimulate my wish for completion as a *feeling* into joy."

Fifth, is the Throat chakra. When *feeling* is trapped here it is expressed as anger. Communication is blocked, the throat may become sore and the thyroid gland affected. All body metabolism becomes disturbed.

Anger is a dominating *feeling*. Its power can make us transcend or it can destroy the physical temple. It is one of the most potent stimuli we have for spiritual growth. It is also the most judged emotion we emit. I could not count the number of times people have told me how badly they felt about getting angry at themselves, another, or at some situation *after* the fact.

Since anger is so powerful, we might remember that the energy of judgment used to repress it must be equally as powerful. Used without judgment anger will lift the body rapidly toward joy. Used with judgment, the body quickly decomposes. Allow anger to flow through without self-condemnation.

Here is an idea about how to prioritize the thinking. "I am angry. I acknowledge this. I accept full responsibility for my anger. In doing so, I do not blame others or judge myself. I *feel* the power it brings as I let it flow through. I now release it to God — the creator of all emotion."

150

Sixth, is the pituitary gland. Its corresponding chakra is called the Brow Chakra or the Third Eye. Here emotional pain is expressed, but does not have to be. The idea of having to suffer in order to progress is an obsolete thought form that is rapidly giving way to new energies.

Pain is the primary reason that people die.

We hold onto pain only because we judge it. An example is, "Why is this happening to me? What have I done to deserve this pain?" Have we ever judged ourself or another? Have we ever said, "My way is higher or better than your way" . . . or "He or she had no right to do that?"

Seventh, we observe the pineal gland. It is a pure lighthouse called the Crown Chakra. It is the receiver and sender of all *feeling* energies coming from below it in the body and above it from God. It encompasses all emotion, all *feeling*. It allows enthusiasm and joy for Life. Opened completely, it can bring total release and total acceptance of Self.

CYCLIC CHAKRA CONNECTIONS

The interesting point about the chakras and the *feeling* states rotating within them is that they are cyclic. They follow the flow of the kundalini. Thus we find that they correspond to each other in a certain cyclic pattern.

The first chakra (gonadal) corresponds to the fifth (thyroid or throat) chakra.

The second chakra (splenic or sacral) corresponds

to the sixth (pituitary).

The third chakra (solar plexus or stomach) corresponds to the seventh (pineal). (See Diagram 5.)

Therefore, when one condemns self by "not knowing" (1st chakra) he correspondingly diminishes the "power" (5th chakra) of the strength to know anything. The ability to manifest anger (5th chakra) is overcome by "not knowing" (1st chakra). When one is climbing out of this self-imposed "unknown" darkness, often anger is expressed.

When one *feels* emotional pain (6th chakra) he many times *feels* physical pain (2nd chakra) and the apathetic complaint of "I can't" dominates the body. Yet as the confusion of physical pain (2nd chakra) climaxes and greater clarity results, the emotional pain (6th chakra) that is pulling this harsh experience up from the sacral area can become the joy (7th chakra) of understanding through *feeling*.

When one *feels* grief or the expressed unworthiness and self-recrimination (3rd chakra) he is pulling on the energies of the 7th chakra where joy and peace will culminate. The 3rd and 7th chakras are also the largest chakras in the body.

The heart chakra is, in my opinion, not just a chakra. It is so unique that we call it a center as mentioned much earlier — the center point of our BEing. It is the area where the Soul Vibration shines through. Therefore, the heart center can appear as a regular chakra if suppressed by fear or a blazing white incandescent sphere if unencumbered. This area fuels all of our life

Diagram 5
CHAKRIC CONNECTIONS

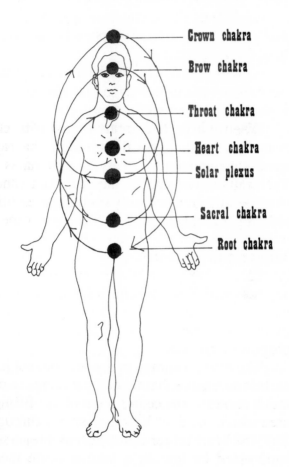

Crown chakra

Brow chakra

Throat chakra

Heart chakra

Solar plexus

Sacral chakra

Root chakra

needs. It is the 4th center. Four is the number of man and completion in numerology. The heart center is that which makes all emotion a possibility no matter how heightened or coarse in vibration.

Only fear can dampen it. For only fear has the ability to retard Soul expression by altering its ability to open completely.

Viewed aurically, the heart chakra may show a diversity of colors, mostly green. However, if the seer looks behind the chakric covering, he will see a brilliant white which is the true heart center. It is rare to see a person with a totally open heart center. However, there are usually moments in every day when this total opening occurs to each of us. I observe this brilliance most often in people when they are helping or in some way selflessly serving another.

THE SUBCHAKRAS

Subchakric energies form the outermost part of the auric field. Their energy flows create perfect auric pyramidal forms of light which correspond to the proportions of the great pyramid at Giza, Egypt. (See diagram 6.) The energy pyramid formed on the crown of the head, acts as a receptor for thought-*feeling* energies. Consequently, these energies feed, sustain, and uplift us.

When *feelings* are of the highest, purest nature, imbued with great joy, enthusiasm and LOVE, then these subchakric pyramids work perfectly and maintain their

Diagram 6
THE SUBCHAKRIC PYRAMIDS

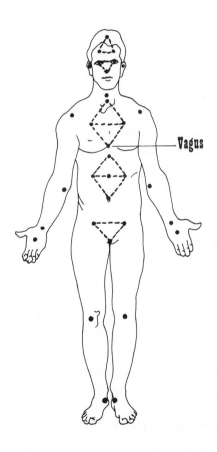

Vagus

correct proportions to the great Egyptian pyramid.

If *feelings* are influenced at all by the ego and allowed to enter the body, the subchakric pyramids will still function. However, the thoughts and emotions, being of an inharmonious nature, alter the energy of the subchakras and thereby change the shape of these energy pyramids. (See Diagram 7.)

Whereas thought-*feelings* of pure joy and enthusiasm contain no elements of matter whatsoever, *egoic feelings* and emotions of lesser light are *not* free of toxic elements and particles of heavier matter.

Minute crystals made of body waste products are constantly being formed in different places in the body as a result of imbalanced thought and emotional processes. The crystals themselves are formed from waste matter which hardens as light enters a *misaligned* subchakric energy pyramid. They are usually very small and hard, and resemble the completely congealed insides of a pimple. The lowered light frequency then combines with these trapped acid wastes and solidifies them. These crystals interfere with the functions of blood, lymph and nerve flow. They are the beginning point of many degenerative processes because of their physiological interference with other structures. Many times these also form damaging adhesions in the body.

As much current research has shown, any crystal has the capacity to store information. (As an example, check your pocket calculators.) The kind of information these crystals contain is what we have chosen to store within them. If there are hurts, fears, angers, jealousies,

Diagram 7
MISALIGNED CHAKRIC PYRAMIDS

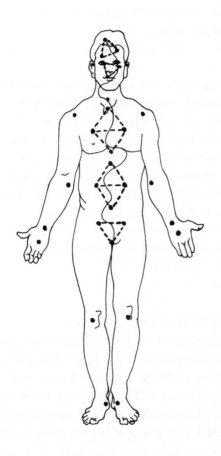

and hates that we don't know how to express, these darker *feelings* will be stored in the crystals. Over lifetimes many crystals still remain within us. These crystalline chips having once again materialized in the body, contain the same dissident *feelings*. Their disturbed vibrations constantly resonating within the auric field form the ego.

Resonances attract their like; we draw people with vibrationally similar ego patterns. What we dislike or resist in another is resonating somewhere within our own hardened crystalline attitudes. In this manner we could recognize our own ego blockages.

The ASCENDED ONES have no crystals, for they have no ego, nor do they make new crystals. They are operating totally within the One Great Law of God. As we begin to operate within this Law, we too will no longer form these crystals within our bodies.

CHAKRA OPENING AND BALANCING

I *feel* it is my duty to caution those who may be attracted to mess around with these practices only for the sake of self-aggrandizement.

The practice of chakra opening and balancing is not new although many would have us believe it to be a phenomenon of these times. It has even become a fad to let someone work on their chakric centers. The tendency is to assume that one or more of our chakras is "shut down." While it is true that some chakras may not be spinning as quickly or as colorfully as others in certain moments, this is a far cry from saying they are "shut down." No aspect of the physical body or its etheric counterparts are completely non-functional as long as life is being expressed in the body. Even a good meal could change their color and rate of spin.

Actually, no one balances or reawakens another's chakras. *It is only the Self that allows inner harmony and awakening.* We are not saying, however, that the presence of another is not beneficial. It can be. By acting as an example to the infirmed one, the spark of balance is rekindled enabling truth to flow into the body.

We are animated by the Soul, the All Powerful I AM Ubiquity. This wholeness quickens all cellular life into motion.

Beware of the quick self-serving way. The pitfalls are deep ravines that we may not be able to climb out of in a lifetime or more. I would therefore question the tampering with chakras in order to *force* one or the other open. I have seen disastrous results from such attempts. The chakras will open and balance in their own time without the aid of rituals or other persons. In reality, chakras are intended to open as naturally as a flower. Let us keep our motive always pure. Exist to serve the highest and best in others at every opportunity. The obvious ways are helping another with some physical or emotional need. A kind word, gesture, or smile, can be as important. For these acts rebalance the chakras and pave the way for their non-traumatic expansion at the exact moment we are ready.

Hold the head of suffering humanity in the lap of loving prayer to God. In the mind's eye, wipe back their tears and as these mingle in the ocean of spacelessness with our *feelings*, so will our chakras blaze in purity.

Chapter 26

PRANA: THE PURIFYING BREATH

Prana is an old Sanskrit word meaning undifferentiated life energy. It fuels the body via the breath. It swirls, twists and shoots through our being every moment of existence in every realm in which we have lived or shall live. It is the amorphous nourishment of the Father.

It is that which pours into and out of the chakras with the cascading force of a waterfall. It animates us. It fires the Soul and quickens all systems in the physical body. When we stifle it, our body begins to wane and age. When we inhale more of it, we begin to animate and return to youth. We must learn to see this mighty force. Here is an exercise for this awakening:

1) On a bright day, pick a point on the horizon where sky meets land. Focus on this for at least one minute.

2) Without removing your eyes from this point, move your vision about one inch above the horizon into the sky.

3) Look for tiny spots of white or translucent light. Begin to notice movement there. At first you may see only their pathways as they seem to dance viva-

ciously in the sky. Remember, they are very tiny. As you start to see a few of them, relax the eyes, but do not go out of focus. Allow your vision to broaden and not just stay at one point or one area.

4) As you expand your sight, you should be able to see many more of these moving whitish dots.

5) Now look about you anywhere in the sky and noticethe hundreds, thousands, millions of thes everywhere. Behold the light and breath of GOD!

So we are surrounded in a measureless ocean of Prana. Never feel alone again. Merely gaze into the sky or onto the face of our beloved and there we will see it dancing endlessly across the waves of eternity.

Life is a series of breaths. **He who only half breathes, only half lives.** To breathe properly is to rhythmically attune the Self, for discord in our daily lives is always reflected in imbalanced breathing patterns.

Most people are mouth breathers which is detrimental to our health. Breathing through the mouth gives but a small portion of the prana we need. This is because of the crucial role that the olfactory (smelling) nerve plays in the process of energy accumulation and distribution. The olfactory nerve is very diverse. It contains many branches. These branches communicate with the brain in a rich manner, carrying energy from the air. Air breathed through the nose thoroughly vitalizes the lungs, enriches the blood and tones the nervous system.

Breathing through the nose also stimulates the kundalini by activation of two nerve branches which start in the nose and terminate in the coccyx (lowest point of the spine). Thus vital energies are constantly spiralling up and down from the brain to the bottom of the spinal cord. In Hindu literature these two nerves are called pingala and ida. Although in modern physiology these nerves are not seen as having any connection or relevance.

This next section shows anatomically how the pingala and ida relate through the first and tenth cranial nerves.

These are the technical facts as traced through *Gray's Anatomy*. First, the olfactory nerve goes directly from the nose into the rhinencephalon (primitive smell center of the brain). Although there are many pathways in the rhinencephalon that are not understood, at least three are. These are the lateral, intermediate and medial olfactory striae. These nerve branches take us through a *very interesting route*:

They go first to the fornix, then the thalamus (emotion center), and finally into the habenular nuclei and commissure which are parts of the stalk that holds the pineal gland. Thus **direct communication is made between proper nose breathing and pineal gland stimulation.** The more energy obtained through nose breathing the more energy is transmitted into the pineal area. From there the mammillotegemental tract of Gudden in the lateral olfactory stria communicates directly with the pons and medulla (breathing center).

The medulla portion of the brain is home to the 10th cranial nerve — the vagus. It is our largest nerve — nicknamed "the wanderer." The vagus connects all nervous systems together. It picks up the energy transmitted via this tract of the olfactory nerve and totally innervates the body. We find the vagus nerve most interfered with by the hiatal hernia syndrome. This is where the stomach ruptures upward through our breathing muscle. The vagus nerve is thus pinched. A plethora of symptoms occur from this. The most common symptom is shortness of breath. Without adequate oxygenation, our foods do not properly assimilate and hydrochloric acid is not sufficiently produced. This equates to a dangerous lack of energy. Many of the people I see afflicted with the hiatal hernia syndrome are mouth breathers.[1]

Here are specific breathing exercises for achieving properly patterned breathing. They may be practiced throughout the day. For when we control our breathing patterns, other conditions inwardly and outwardly start to hone into a harmonious focus. An old Hindu adage goes: "Consciousness is like a kite, and breath is the string."

We will begin by understanding the **Complete**

1   More on this subject is available in my book, <u>Hiatal Hernia Syndrome: Insidious Link to Major Illness</u>.

164

Breath. It is suggested that you learn this while lying on your back. After you have grasped it, then stand and practice it. Inhalation can be divided into three parts:

1) Inhale into the lower abdomen. Let the belly rise outward as you inhale down into this area. Exhale through the nose. Practice alone ten times then rest.

2) Breathe into your middle area. This is just below the end of the chest. You will feel a little bone there. This is called the xyphoid process. Expand outward ten times. Exhale through the nose, then rest.

3) Breathe into your upper chest. Be sure to feel your collarbone (clavicles) rise. Expand outward ten times. Exhale through the nose, then rest. This part should present no difficulty as this is where most people breathe from most of the time.

4) Combine these three in a complete breath. Expand from the bottom (abdomen), then into the middle (stomach), then into the upper chest, lifting the collarbones. Exhale by pushing out the breath through the nose down into the abdomen. Reach the pubic bone area if possible.

5) Inhale again starting from the abdomen, then ex-

panding the stomach and finally the chest. Practice this five times; then rest. You may feel light-headed at first, but this is normal.

Next to learn is the **Cleansing Breath**. This exercise ventilates and cleanses the lungs reducing fatigue.

1) Inhale a complete breath as described above.

2) Hold the air for several seconds.

3) Pucker the lips as if whistling. Vigorously exhale through the mouth a little air at a time. Stop for a moment then exhale more.

4) Repeat until all air is exhaled. Do it at least 3 times. You should *feel* refreshed.

Another important exercise is called the **Rhythmic Breath**.

1) Inhale a complete breath reaching your maximum capacity in six heartbeats.

2) Hold this breath for three beats.

3) Exhale to your maximum in six beats.

4) Hold air out for three beats.

5) Repeat seven times.

This is a powerful stimulant to the liver, pancreas, and stomach. Feel free to use it as much as you need. This one can be practiced while walking as well. Breathe in for six steps. Hold air for three steps then exhale for six steps and hold air out for three more steps.

Lastly is the **Grand Breath**. This is important because of the total vitality it imparts to the system.

1) Lying on your back, inhale a complete breath. Start with your feet and see this breath being drawn into the very bone marrow and all surrounding tissues. When exhaling, visualize the bones and tissues as doing this. Go through each part of the body. See each part inhaling this total energy and exhaling any waste products.

2) After inhaling and exhaling through all the bones and tissues, begin this same procedure with the chakras. Start with the crown chakra and go down through all seven into the root chakra at the base of the spine. (See Diagram 4 for chakra locations.)

Throughout the day, it will be noted that we breathe through one nostril more than the other. This is normal. Occasionally while doing the exercise on rhythmic breath it is good to hold one nostril closed and breathe just through that one. This has different effects on the nervous system all of which are beneficial.

Pick any or all of these breathing exercises and see how they work. The practice of rhythmic breathing is an incredible impetus in gaining eternal life.

Chapter 27

DIET FOR PURIFICATION

The body is the temple of God. How will you treat the temple? To LOVE God, LOVE HIS temple.

Even the perfect diet does not guarantee ASCENSION. Only total and complete *feeling* immersed in the One Great Law of God will lead to body vibrations becoming so high, so fine and so quick as to turn the body to light and transmute eternally.

There are no 'exacts' when it comes to diet. However, in most cases, the body will be aided by improved diet. For it helps in the elimination of heavy mucous forming toxins that impairs light coming into the body. This assists the body's quest for proper digestive action and better caloric food energy dispersion throughout the individual cells.

FOOD COMBINING

Eating poor foods in poor combinations reduces the light in each cell. (See Appendix for diagram and full dietary recommendations.) If the digestive system is strong, adherence to food combining is less necessary. If the system is weak, attention to food combining becomes imperative. Many of our foods (even organically grown) are nutrient deficient. This makes them even harder to absorb so proper combining is of greater importance. The more nutrients in proper proportion, the more light per cell; and the more light per cell, the greater the chances for transmutation.

ACID-ALKALINE BALANCE

There are certain ratios of acid to alkaline that the human body functions with. These are notably eighty percent (80%) alkaline forming and twenty percent (20%) acid forming foods. These ideal ratios assist elimination of mucous, and increase health. (See Appendix for further dietary recommendations.)

DIET

This diet may not be what the usual dietary consultant or doctor might suggest. It is not meant only to help us *feel* better (although we will feel quite a bit better), nor are we speaking of improving our health just to "get by." We are speaking of ASCENSION, of laying the physical groundwork for *total feeling*. (See Appendix for full diet of Transmutation and ASCENSION.)

CLEANSING

The first goal is elimination of poisons that have settled between the cellular tissue levels throughout the entire body. For when we purify on the physical/cellular level all levels are affected. We clean the cobwebs of disease from our bodies and thus transmute the dark corners of our emotions to sparkling light.

Finally, it is possible to transcend the need for *any* nutritional aids and procedures. What is necessary is that we allow ourselves to *feel* worthy enough to transmute any and all toxic wastes in our body to pure light. Prayer at mealtime greatly increases the energy in the food we eat.

It is not my wish to create another "ism," another system for us dogmatically and nonsensically to follow. If we become an unhappy slave to these dietary suggestions instead of expressing joy, then we are defeating the intended purpose in following them.

Use intuition. Follow these suggestions only if the God-Self *feels* good about them.

Chapter 28

THE HEALING HEAT

Our characteristic diet of emotions, thoughts, and words are equally important as our diet of food. As they are constructively changed, however, consciousness is vibrationally raised leading to a healing heat process or crisis, even on a subtle level.

Toxins break loose in the body and move through the blood and lymph system into the colon, skin, and kidneys for final removal. If the body does *not* eliminate these dead attitudinal toxins quickly enough it produces heat and discomfort in some of these areas.

The effects of this healing process are different from what might have been experienced in a purely physical regime of cleansing. We are learning to *feel* through the pain, fever and confusion a healing process can bring. The healing heat is actually the burning off of old ego constructs; vanity and/or unworthiness. It comes as a result of certain self-inflicted cruelties that limited us in the past. We are now being freed of these via this heat of increasing consciousness. Rejoice!

Many times the body cleans itself in exactly the reverse order of the illnesses it has experienced. Although the process might express as a neighborhood flu, I have noticed a different phenomenon occurring within the auric field of those who are working to upgrade the body for Transmutation and ASCENSION and those who are not. In the third layer of the auric pattern, a green color manifests itself. If you are not seeing auras at this point, there are two other ways to confirm a healing heat. The first is to have a professional iridologist look at your irises. He or he will see a whiteness appearing throughout the eye that may also look slightly cloudy. This disappears when the heat subsides. Eye color may also be slightly changed.

Another way to test for a healing process is with a kinesiological test. Use either food enzymes, liquid minerals, Bio-Strath®, or any of the substances given in the Appendix to do this. To begin, have the person you are testing for the healing process to extend his arm. Press down on the arm for strength. Just test it to see if is firm. If not use the other arm. Have the person being tested hold an opened bottle of nutritional supplements next to the solar plexus area. Now test the strong arm again while the person is holding the substance. If the arm goes weak, the person in question is truly in a healing process. This is a simple one minute test that works. Remember to congratulate them if they are, no matter how puny they *feel*.

During these healing heats one may *feel* the need to sleep more. For while experiencing micro beatings of small disruptive *feelings* all day long, the body yearns to rest and repair itself by ridding through sleep the excess acid residues that they bring. For even the least *feeling* of anger, frustration, jealousy, greed, unworthiness, fear or vanity, inflicts a toll on our body cells. The more intense these dissident *feelings* are expressed the greater

174

the damage to our many body systems.

Even the minutest thought of discord toward another causes punishment to the body. Have you ever been thinking (*feeling*) along some clearly delineated path and suddenly from out of nowhere a discordant thought about someone or something else bursts into your mind? This dissident thought, which is *feeling*, disrupts your original pure thought-*feeling*. Even these minor incidences wear the body energies down and disturb its processes at the cellular level and can damage the genetic structure. Sleep is the body's method of recovering from the ravages of *feelings* less than total joy, peace and enthusiasm.

Ultimately, we never need to sleep. For joy, peace, and enthusiasm build and vitalize the body systems. Occasionally we see or hear of advanced Souls who no longer need to sleep. The ego is not standing in between their connection to their "heart center." So these persons simply stay in contact with this endless source of *feeling* and vitality that exists within. Increased *feeling* equals increased heat as long as any vestige of balance is needed in the body.

ASCENSION is beyond balance. There is only joy and continued growth. There is only the total expression of the One Great Law. There is only openness and receptivity to more LOVE. Balance becomes a secure place for insecure people. We are truly stable after we ASCEND.

Let go and grow. We will be more clear-headed, more stable and more sure of ourselves. We will gain a

175

poise that is unmistakable. It's the mark of one who is allowing himself to realize the ASCENDED STATE. Serenity of heart is not escape from the storms of life, but the finding of peace within those gales.

Jesus said, "I come not to bring peace but a sword." He came to stir our hearts and bring them out of their lethargy toward the ASCENSION. The healing fire may be experienced often on this zestful journey. In between these episodes of growth will be increased health of mind and spirit because we will be ready to grasp a new star. When the healing processes are finished, the ego is reintegrated in the auric field and purification is complete.

Part V

STAGES OF BLOOMING

Chapter 29

STAGE IV - THE BUD: TRANSMUTATION

One of the most powerful forces in any universe is the awesome *feeling* that propels the growing stem of a plant to bud. It is complete, all-consuming, one-pointed. The bud is literally tearing out of its final prison with wordless joy. In us it is only experienced when every sinew of our BEing totally *feels* — is totally alive. This is called — **Transmutation.**

It is a moment of increased latitude. It is a beginning of comprehensive independence. It is a time of inestimable power. For no longer are we limited by gravity of the Earth. We have become an incandescent transformer of indescribable joy. In the budding stage of Transmutation all bonds shift. Attitudes that once held us in thralldom do so no longer.

As the bud slowly changes before it blooms, so this stage is characterized by several minor stages within itself.

RECOGNIZING TRANSMUTATIVE EXPERIENCES

These can be recognized during a Lucid Sprouting (Stage II) when we are conscious in another realm. For an interesting thing happens to the physical body when we are conscious in another realm even for a few moments. This is known in other terms as an 'out-of-body' experience in which we totally leave our earthly body behind in the 4th realm. In truth, it is an extension of our molecular structure strung from one realm to the next. An actual part of our physical body provides the energy to manifest a form that is a duplicate of ourself in another dimension.

This is called a "simultaneous existence" as described previously in Chapter 18, and stays there as long as we are consciously aware of solidly being in that dimension. When energy wanes or something disturbs us in this 4th realm Earth dimension, we snap across "x" number of dimensions back into this one. Our molecules also return and reintegrate parts of the ego at that time.

CLASSIFYING TRANSMUTATIVE EXPERIENCES

When the physical body and spiritual being are pure enough, then we can transmute all of the physical body to any place. This is a full Transmutation. At that instant we have fully entered this extremely powerful Stage IV. We become the tender, yet forceful, bud that begins its ripening upon the well developed stalk that the Purification provided. For any experience that changes the physical body from matter to light then rematerializes wherever it is willed by the transmuter is to be considered complete Transmutation. This may be as simple as transmuting our physical form and moving it to the next room or moving across the planet and rematerializing. It also includes transmuting the body and rematerializing it in the 12th realm.

The Budding Stage is so compelling that its very light can distract our attention. Thus, we must learn to control the process and like water, seek our own level. The more we LOVE, the more control we can have to transmute. Where we end up is entirely dependent upon the amount of energy, via *feeling*, we generate.

Just as in the Lucid Sprouting Stage, we must first learn to crawl. The more we practice, the better we get. There is no hurry and every day provides opportunities to learn another nuance of the process. When we *feel* comfortable moving from San Francisco to Miami in the blink of an eye, we will be ready to go from New York City to Lhasa, Tibet.

SEPARATING TRANSMUTATION FROM ASCENSION

Many times when one first transmutes the body there will be a period of going and coming within the realms. In some schools of thought, this is called AS-CENSION. The difference between a Transmutation and the blessed ASCENSION (Stage V) is ASCEN-SION is beyond matter, time and space. Whereas when experiencing Transmutation, it is still possible to come back rather soon to this 4th realm. In ASCENSION this is possible too. However, there is an adjustment period that might take a few earth years before we could final-ly return here, remanifest a physical form and visit our

181

friends again. This occurs because of the radica
molecular changes and the preparation for adjusting t
a matter body in this heavier realm.

As pure as the Transmutation Budding Stage is i
comparison to most of those in which we function, it i
still within the realms, therefore within the areas o
time, space, matter, and ego. Even in this exalted stage
we might find ourselves the hapless victims of a bit o
ego. However, let it be well noted, that this is not of th
same nature as found in any of the three previous stage:
The tests of ego and lessons of LOVE that are learne
at this level are of a subtle and wondrous nature.

EXERCISE FOR TRANSMUTATION

To further *feel* Transmutation, harmonize the ac
tivity between body and Soul. The following exercis
will produce results. Twenty to thirty minutes will b
needed at night before going to bed and in the mornin
before starting the day's work.

1) Be certain you are not disturbed by phones or pet

2) Sit in a comfortable chair or on the floor. N
specific posture is necessary. Just get as comfor
able as you can.

3) Close your eyes and breathe in and out deeply a fe
times.

4) After settling down and becoming very still, pictur

and *feel* your body surrounded in a brilliant white light.

5) For the first five to seven minutes or so, intensely *feel* your connection between the outer-self and your I AM self within the heart center.

6) Visualize the heart center as a star of even brighter white than the light around you.

7) Next, intensify this great light and *feel* this in every cell of your body for ten minutes more.

8) Close this exercise with this affirmation or create your own: "I am a child of God. I live in Its great light. I serve this light. I am surrounded, guarded and LOVED within this light at all moments."

This is a very powerful prayer/meditation exercise. If practiced diligently it will yield excellent results.

Physical exercise also plays a tremendous role in Transmutation. Daily workouts are recommended. As we exercise, our bodies are oxygenated and alkalized which is necessary for a complete Transmutation.

I am suggesting no particular regimen of exercise. Use intuition to pick that which suits your body type. It could be as simple as walking or as complicated as some of the Oriental martial arts. Each exercise session becomes a small Transmutation of the body, for toxic wastes are stirred out of the cells and more light enters into the crown chakra.

Also use intuition to tell you when to stop exercising! If you overdo it, harmony is altered.

FREQUENCIES OF TRANSMUTATION

When asking about rates of frequency concerning the Realms of Transmutation I was given this by a member of the Brotherhood: "We of the Brotherhood are in the 12th realm - 7th dimension. In other words, the 139th dimension. The realms end after the 144th dimension. For us to enter into the ASCENDED states where no time and space exist, we would have to increase the spinning of our individual energy cycles by 360 times."

Be not discouraged by this prospect nor think the achievement of Transmutation and ASCENSION such a challenge. In truth, it is much easier than choosing to die (the unnecessary occurrence).

A concept called the Fibonacci Relationship, that helps us understand how much easier Transmutation is than we really think was developed by an Italian named Fibonacci. He discovered many years ago an important mathematical equation.

Essentially what it tells us is how we accumulate energy within the Realms of Transmutation by allowing greater LOVE within us. It is a numerical description of what is sometimes called the "golden ratio" or "golden spiral." It denotes the density of matter in a particular realm in arithmatic progression.

Once we start building our energies of LOVE i

takes less and less to accomplish more and more. Spiritual growth or understanding of the One Great Law is a geometric affair. In other words, we do not climb in an organized linear manner, but we expand geometrically. We start at square one, then go to square two, then square four, then square sixteen, then square thirty-two, etc. It is this type of geometric progression which all spiritual evolution follows. We expand in leaps, according to our heartfelt desire to LOVE the Self.

Let us look at the way Fibonacci determines this geometric energy relationship.

Fibonacci discovered that many relationships in mathematics express themselves thus: By adding two numbers together at a starting point of zero plus zero, $(0 + 0 = 0)$. Zero is a number that has weight and mass. Now to proceed with $0 + 1 = 1$. The total of $0 + 0$ being zero, the zero is taken as the first part of the next step, thus zero plus one equals one. Now the one as a total is taken as the beginning of the next step and becomes $(1 + 1 = 2)$. The two as the total of that step is put in front of the next step and $2 + 1 = 3$.

To continue, the total of three combines with the previous beginning equation number of two from $2 + 1 = 3$ and the 3 combines with the two making $3 + 2 = 5$. The next step following the same progression takes the total 5 and adds this to the previous equation's first number three, thus we have $5 + 3 = 8$. Again, 8 becomes the first part of the next step and five becomes the second part making it $8 + 5 = 13$.

185

Now that we have an understanding of this progression, we will take this and apply it to the geometry of the Realms of Transmutation.

The 12th realm contains the least density within all the realms, therefore it follows that the lowest numbers of weight and mass apply to this realm. So we begin with:

$$0 + 0 = 0 = \text{12th Realm}$$

$$0 + 1 = 1 = \text{11th Realm}$$

$$1 + 1 = 2 = \text{10th Realm}$$

$$2 + 1 = 3 = \text{9th Realm}$$

$$3 + 2 = 5 = \text{8th Realm}$$

$$5 + 3 = 8 = \text{7th Realm}$$

$$8 + 5 = 13 = \text{6th Realm}$$

$$13 + 8 = 21 = \text{5th Realm}$$

$$21 + 13 = 34 = \text{4th Realm}$$

$$34 + 21 = 55 = \text{3rd Realm}$$

$$55 + 34 = 89 = \text{2nd Realm}$$

$$89 + 55 = 144 = \text{1st Realm}$$

Notice how the densities of matter in relationships to these numbers change from realm to realm. One must produce quite a volume of LOVE to transmute between the 1st realm and the 2nd realm, equal to 55 units. For one to transmute from the 2nd realm to the 3rd realm requires only 34 units. And so it goes becoming less and less of an energy expenditure, which is the amount of LOVE you can generate, to transmute from realm to realm. Look at your advantages being in the 4th realm. The amount of energy (LOVE) required to move through these realms is not as great as one might think. Then what is holding us back? Our lack of absolute knowingness through *feeling* that we are capable and worthy of LOVING ourself into the next realm.

Does this explanation make our ability to enter into the budding Transmutation Stage seem a little more possible? It should.

Consider this: The generation of just a little more *feeling* than we have previously allowed ourself is the blasting cap that skyrockets us into the next dimension. Only 13 units of energy separate us from transmuting our body to light and entering with the body into the 5th realm. From there onward, even fewer. The Brotherhoods of Light agree that the Fibonacci relationships do point out energy similarities between the realms.

In essence, we are a great deal closer to ASCENDING than previously thought. Let us calculate further with these numbers. To go the distance between the 4th and 5th realms is a matter of 13 units. In the Pythagorean system of numerology the number 13 is interpreted as

$1 + 3 = 4$. Four is a number of completion to the Pythagoreans and we are living in the 4th realm. Could it be that the ASCENDED Pythagoras understood this relationship of numbers leading to ASCENSION for those on this dimension? Could his understanding of this be one of the reasons *he* ASCENDED?

The Transmutation is always a ripe bud that is about to burst with stupendous power into a full bloom. As it crowns its stalk, it is at once a power that *IS* and a force of boundless irresistible thrust to *BE*.

Such is the One Great Law of God which supports and sustains this bud. And such are we — the prime aspirant for this illumined state.

Chapter 30

CYCLES OF TRANSMUTATION

We are a wondrous blending of many beauteous cycles. They are ribbon-like bands of energy within the aura. In most of us the majority of these cycles are latent or not operating fully. As they activate, usually one at a time, the body is being cleansed of toxins. Self-destructive unworthiness attitudes are being transformed and reintegrated into the God Self.

There are approximately 12 to 15 major cycles in the human aura, with many minor cycles in between. The total number of all, major and minor, is 360, which is the reason a circle has 360 degrees and the circle is a symbol of wholeness for mankind. When all are fully activated and spinning in perfect white light harmony, transmutation of the physical body into the next dimension occurs. (See Diagram 7.)

Between each major cycle lie many minor cycles, sometimes up to thirty. This varies according to how many major cycles there are. All of the minor cycles must be activated between each major cycle before a *new* major cycle will permanently activate.

It is common, however, that we may get an inkling of a new major cycle that we are working toward before we get there. This activation will last only a little while and we will have a brief period of elation. However, until all the minor cycles between have activated, the major cycle activated early will not stabilize permanently for our use and spiritual growth.

How is a new cycle awakened? What exactly happens as it cleanses or detoxifies? As a cycle begins its sluggish change, bits and pieces of toxic matter are flung off, perhaps never to be trapped upon it again. Eventually it will synchronize itself with the other cycles and new energies are *felt*. These are sometimes referred to as spiritual gifts, such as telepathy, clairvoyance, clairaudience, understanding and perception of time and its cycles, awareness of lucid experiencing through simultaneous existences, and the meeting of our guides and Oversouls.

These cycles become more harmonious as they are toned up, much as we tone up our muscles. The best toning occurs when total joy and enthusiasm have been experienced in some aspect of our lives.

All knowledge of Self is available within the aura, and the cycles unite all aspects of the chakras with the aura, making this information possible to be retrieved. The clearer, cleaner, and more active each cycle, the better the information we can recover or remember from our pasts and futures. Also, we will be able to see, hear, smell and taste with a higher intuitive ability.

As all 360 of these cycles slowly begin to roll into motion about the individual, a very fascinating occurrence begins. The physical body becomes more and more alkaline in nature. A substance called *chyle*, is produced in greater measure by the liver, the peyers patches of the small intestine, and other lymph glands throughout the body.

Chyle (sometimes called golden globules) is the major alkalizing force in our bodies. The more chyle produced, the higher becomes the overall body vibrations. If enough chyle is produced, the body will begin to etherealize. In other words, it will disappear from 4th realm vision. This happens only when all the cycles are almost completely acid or toxic free.

Next, an enzyme called *transmutase* is produced. It is the exact etheric equivalent to the physical substance chyle. The more chyle produced, the more *transmutase* produced. *Transmutase* looks like silver pieces of tin foil floating about in the auric field. The closer we get to an actual Transmutation, the more *transmutase* is seen and the brighter it becomes.

As each cell is completely alkalized, tremendous light is created. For this desire to LOVE draws the indestructible, everlasting units of energy called *electrons* closer and closer into the nucleus of each atom in each cell of our body. These electrons create great energy by their rapid spinning and all toxins and ego thoughts that might have heretofore slowed this spin with their heavy matter is now cast off and transmuted, atom by atom, to pure light and brilliance. This ignites greater portions of *transmutase* from its silver fleck form into a solid illumination of unspeakably beautiful white, warm light. We simply vanish from this dimension and appear in another of less density.

An alkalization of the body has been created and the physiology of Transmutation is complete.

191

Chapter 31

THE ISLES OF ASCENSION

An Isle is a band of vibrational frequency similar to the realms—with one major difference. The Isles are vibrating at such a rate that the heavier components of time, space and matter are completely transcended. Time and space simply dissolve at these frequencies. Hence, the term "beyond time and space."

The Isles of ASCENSION are constantly floating. They never stagnate. There are countless numbers of these Isles and multitudes of overall inhabitants. These are the ASCENDED ONES. They live in the light of God and the One Great Law. They stand as perfect examples of LOVE.

Unlike the realms, the Isles are not set in dimensions. They are states of consciousness each within itself. The ASCENDED ONES call them 'knots.' In olden times when an initiate of spiritual pursuit attained a certain status and was recognized by his teacher, he was given a knot tied in a rope to wear around his waist like a belt. The more knots, the greater the wisdom and understanding had been gained.

It is important to know that there are levels to AS-CENSION that occur within the Isles just as there are levels to the process of Transmutation that occur within the realms. Within the Isles, where ego is non-existent,

there are always deeper levels of *feeling*. This process of
LOVING in a totality of unlimited *feeling* has no beginning or end.

To experience the Isles is like looking in a mirror
which reflects our every thought totally manifested. The
ASCENDED ONES allowed me a personal experience
so that I could better understand this.

I saw at the very end of the realms a
line of crystalline forms which separated
the dimensional areas from the non-dimen-
sional Isles. As these energies from the
Isles encountered the crystalline forms
there was great friction and the appearance
of flame produced. This is known as the
Sacred Fire which all must pass through
when ASCENDING.

I then gazed upon the Isles where
luminous castles were floating on whitish
land masses. Each castle and Isle had a
color around it — green, blue, yellow, etc.,
with an aura of white around that. One of
the inhabitants explained to me that the
principal way they differentiated themselves is by these colors. The Isles and their
diverse abodes floated in a sea of mist so
that one Isle seemed to float below or above
the other. The mist itself was sometimes
violet, blue, green, or yellow, with billions
of brilliant specks like stars. There are no

adjectives to describe such luminosity.

I also saw golden gates, beautiful but unusual trees, and portals shaped like doughnuts. I peered through them and found myself in different locations. After that I was escorted back to this realm by an ASCENDED ONE.

I then asked what I might see beyond the Isles if I traveled into the heart of God. The reply was, "You would see yourself."

Chapter 32

THE CYCLES OF ASCENSION

There are 33 major ASCENSION cycles. Is it any wonder why this important number appears so often in relation to spiritual teaching? And they are the same for everyone.

The total number of cycles, including the minor AS-CENSION cycles, is 360. This means there are approximately ten or eleven minor cycles between each major ASCENSION cycle. These minor cycles must be activated between the opening of each new major AS-CENSION cycle.

There are five steps in the activation of the major ASCENSION cycles, arranged in groups of eight cycles per step. That is: eight cycles times four steps equals 32 cycles, with the fifth step containing only one cycle, totalling 33.

An initial difference between these ASCENSION cycles and the Transmutation cycles is that all ASCEN-SION cycles start out completely white. The Transmutation cycles must activate and spin harmoniously until all toxic attitudes and bodily conditions are reintegrated. Then these Transmutation cycles will also spin white.

Even without having a complete Transmutative experience, a few cycles could be activated. In fact, it is quite possible to begin activation of the 33 cycles while still in the Purification stage. Total activation of these ASCENSION cycles is only part of what is necessary — they must also run in a harmonious pattern with the Transmutation cycles.

How will we know we have activated any of the AS-CENSION cycles? At times when *feeling* a tremendous amount of LOVE and joy about something, some of these cycles may be momentarily activated. Have you ever *felt* so happy that you were walking on air? This is a moment when many Transmutation and ASCEN-SION cycles are spinning in harmony. This is when, if you but knew how, you could bring about a complete Transmutation. All that limits us is doubt and fear that we are unworthy of this. We are worthy. It has been within our grasp many times if we had but recognized it.

As the ASCENSION cycles activate by ever-increasing *feeling*, the ASCENDED ONES classify them thus:

1)   The first 8 cycles are the Initiation of Light.

2)   The second 8 cycles are the Initiation of Fire.

3)   The third 8 cycles are the Initiation of Grounding.

4)   The fourth 8 cycles are the Initiation of Sound.

The remaining cycle is like dynamite that blasts into action all 33. It is the ultimate flame of white, infused with a light blue mist so brilliant that its edges seem to cut the sight with the magnificence of its pureness. Thi last cycle, called the Initiation of Total Purity, is activated by God. It is final acknowledgment and acceptance into the Isles of ASCENSION.

Chapter 33

STAGE V - THE BLOOM: ASCENSION

Definition of the
Pythagorean Master Number 33

THE ADEPT

The fact of Immortality is attained in his physical body. The omnipotence of the One Great Law of LOVE is realized. He becomes a Lord of Compassion.

There are biochemical and electronic aspects of ASCENSION.

STAGE I

1) When we *feel* the One Great Law of LOVE without resistance, the alkaline enzyme, chyle is instantly produced throughout the physical body, especially in the peyers patches of the small intestines.

2) As greater *feelings* of LOVE permeate the body a wondrous cycle begins. More alkaline chyle enzymes are produced which in turn lead to a greater capacity to *feel* LOVE.

STAGE II

3) As more chyle is secreted, more transmutase ions are created chemically. This produces the silver specks of the transmutase enzyme. Their silver color denotes that they are not yet activated.

STAGE III

4) Assuming no toxins exist to stop the process, and more enthusiasm is generated, the chyle begins to saturate every level. When this happens the Transmutation cycles start activation and come into harmony.

STAGE IV

5) As they come into harmony, the enzyme chyle is increased throughout the body. This speeding of the Transmutation cycles causes transmutase enzymes to change from an inactive silver color to brilliant white light. This is accomplished by having greater *feelings* of joy generated for Self and God. The body begins to take on a 'glow' as this profuse amount of chyle continues to convert chemically to white transmutase. The body then disappears from physical sight.

6) Being transmuted to a state of elevated freedom

throughout the realms, the process continues toward ASCENSION. Just as chyle became the base for the etheric enzyme transmutase, transmutase now becomes the base for another even more potent etheric enzyme —*piloramase*. *Piloramase* is produced within the biochemical electronic structure of the perfect etheric double. Whereas the etheric enzyme transmutase is silver until completely aligned, the enzyme *piloramase* is white from the beginning. So the process develops from chyle to transmutase to piloramase enzymes.

STAGE V

7) As the perfect double becomes infused with yet greater energy, the enzyme piloramase ionically changes from inactive white to a brilliant white activating all ASCENSION cycles.

8) With this full illumination and activation of the physical body and its perfect double, ASCENSION occurs in a blazing moment. . . .

And is ASCENSION the end? Of course not. Better to say it is a beginning! For God is ever expanding through us. There are even greater cycles of light and magnitude awaiting us beyond the glorious ASCENSION cycles.

The coming of the Christ Consciousness is the beacon to ASCENSION. Death is becoming old fashioned. Live forever in the state of endless Joy. BE the ASCENDED ONE.

Master all heavens. *Feel* the singular destiny that will not change, that only awaits our complete embrace. LOVE the Self impeccably and ASCEND.

Thus ends this long prayer.

I am Myself. And because of this I become unto
the earth a beacon of shining Light.

I am Light. And because of this I warm the earth
With the intensity of Life.

I am Life. And because of this I transmute all feelings of transgression into Peace.

I am Peace. And because of this I fly throughout
the nations and manifest Joy.

I am Joy. And because of this the oneness of feeling flowers within me into pure Love.

I am Love. And because of this I transform the intensity of all Light, Peace and Joy into the Oneness
of God.

I am God. And because of this I recognize the
reality of Myself.

I am Myself. And because of this I Ascend
All dualities that I AM.

I AM. . . .

Rose Marie Baroody

APPENDIX

This section is the synthesis of great study, observation of thousands of patients, and extensive discussions with many spiritual Brotherhoods and ASCENDED ONES.

FOOD COMBINING

If proteins are mixed with starches such as meat and potatoes or meat and rice in the same meal, they putrefy. This is because the enzymes and hydrochloric acid necessary to digest these foods become active at different times and when both are ingested together one set of digestive interactions cancels out the other. Then all you have is a glob of chewed up, poorly digested food. This produces acid waste products, blocks light receptivity to higher consciousness, leads to body electron dispersal, and ultimately, death.

The next improper combination is fruits and vegetables. When combined together in the same meal, they ferment. It is suggested that you read other books for a fuller explanation if you desire an in-depth chemical understanding. Simply stated, the timing and enzyme action is different for fruits than for vegetables. Eat fruit about thirty minutes to an hour before a vegetable meal. That way the fruit will not interfere with proper assimilation of nutrients to each cell.

Another improper combination is proteins and

207

Diagram 8
Food Combining

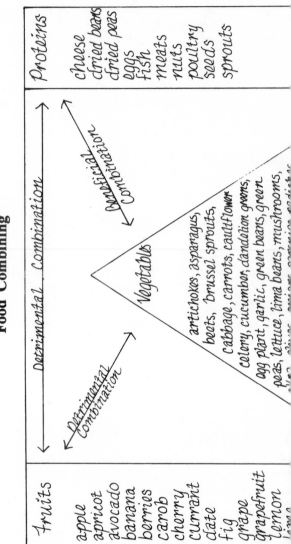

← Detrimental Combination →

← Detrimental Combination →

← Beneficial Combination →

Fruits

apple
apricot
avocado
banana
berries
carob
cherry
currant
date
fig
grape
grapefruit
lemon
lime

Vegetables

artichokes, asparagus,
beets, brussel sprouts,
cabbage, carrots, cauliflower
celery, cucumber, dandelion greens,
egg plant, garlic, green beans, green
peas, lettuce, lima beans, mushrooms,
okra, onions, parsnips, radishes

Proteins

cheese
dried beans
dried peas
eggs
fish
meats
nuts
poultry
seeds
sprouts

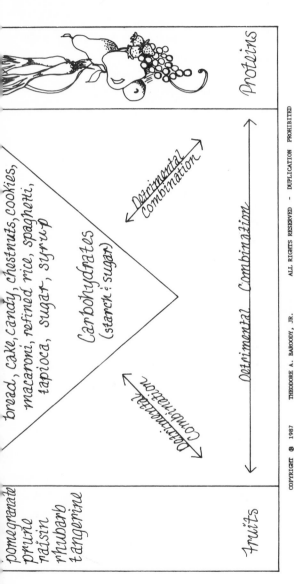

Proteins

bread, cake, candy, chestnuts, cookies,
macaroni, refined rice, spaghetti,
tapioca, sugar, syrup

Carbohydrates
(starch & sugar)

pomegranate
prune
raisin
rhubarb
tangerine

Fruits

Detrimental
Combination

Detrimental
Combination

Detrimental Combination

fruits such as meat and fruit salad. The same reasoning applies to this category as the aforementioned categories. Fruit stops the action of necessary hydrochloric acid and pepsinogen production when meat is simultaneously added to it and the whole mess putrifies.

"Holy baloney! What can I eat?" you ask. First of all, avoid the baloney. It is full of preservatives and diverse processed animal parts that would not meet your immediate approval if you knew what you were eating.

We can successfully mix proteins and vegetables. Hoorah! We can successfully mix starches and vegetables. Another milestone! Imagine God being so clever.

One option for breakfast is to just eat fruit. Another option is wheatless waffles or pancakes. A highly nutritious combination is to mix sugarless organic granola with banana milk. Banana milk is made by using a ripe banana and blending it with a little water and ice and adding a bit of honey if not sweet enough. Then pour the banana milk over the granola. This seems to be quite an agreeable combination and gives the cereal eaters a safe way to eat without the use of homogenized milk.

If we dump fruit into the system between our noon-time meal and our eveningtime meal, there is a good possibility that the slower digesting proteins and vegetables may not have totally emptied out. Therefore the fruit ingested between these two meals may cause a fermentative or putrefactive process. Eat fruits alone or as suggested about thirty minutes to an hour before a meal.

Eating dried fruit with nuts is certainly an exception to the rule of proteins and fruits. The contents of dry fruit does not interfere as greatly with the digestive activity necessary for digesting the nuts (proteins).

Melons are wondrous food. Because of their rapid digestion time and high amount of self-contained enzymes it is recommended that they be eaten separately.

There are certain minor exceptions to all of these rules, but they are indeed minor. For the most part, what is outlined here, are more wholesome combinations to take into the body.

ACID-ALKALINE BALANCE

Arranging our foods according to the ratios of 20% acid forming and 80% alkaline forming, obeys certain physical biochemical laws. (See diagram.) It is further recommended that our foods be 75% fresh and raw and 25% cooked per day. Ease into these ratios. Too much too quick can be physically uncomfortable. We might start comfortably with 60% fresh and raw foods and 40% cooked.

Diagram 9

ACID AND ALKALINE FOOD LIST

The body seems to work best on a high ratio of alkaline-forming foods — those foods which give alkaline elements when broken down by digestion. A diet which contains 70-80% alkaline forming food is ideal for healthful living.

FRUITS

Acid — Blueberries, coconut, cranberries (unless mixed with 1/2 water), Damson plums, dried fruit, canned fruit, jams, jellies sugared and sulphured fruits.

Alkaline — All other fresh fruits and fresh juices: Apples, apricots avocado, bananas, berries, cherries, currants, figs, grapes grapefruit, kiwi, lemons, limes, melons, nectarine, oranges, papaya peaches, pears, persimmons, pineapple, plum, pomegranate prunes, pumpkin, raisins, raspberry, sour grape, strawberries tangerines, tomatoes, watermelon.

VEGETABLES

Acid — Ginger, sweet potatoes.

Alkaline — All other fresh vegetables: artichokes, asparagus, bamboo shoots, beets, broccoli, brussel sprouts, cabbage, carrot cauliflower, celery, collards, corn (sweet), cucumbers, daikon, dandelion greens, eggplant, endive, escarole, garlic, horseradish, kale kelp, leeks, lettuces, mushrooms, okra, olives, onions, parsley parsnips, peas, peppers, potatoes (if eaten with skins), radishe rhubarb, rutabaga, sauerkraut, spinach, summer squash, swiss chard, taro, turnips, watercress, winter squash.

GRAINS

Acid — Barley, brown rice, oats, rye berries, wheat berries.

Alkaline — Buckwheat, corn (dry), millet, quinoa. Any grain that sprouted is alkaline.

MEATS/PROTEINS

Acid — Beef, fowl, game, lamb, pork, and other meats, fish, egg cheeses.

Alkaline — Acidophilus, raw milk, whey, yogurt (with no sugar).

Neutral — Butter, cream, margarine.

BEANS

Acid – Aduki, black, garbanzo, kidney, lentils, navy, red, white and any other dried beans.
Alkaline – Green, lima, fresh peas, snap, soybeans, string, and all sprouted dry beans.

STARCHES

Acid – Bran, breads, cereals, cornstarch, crackers, custards, flours, oatmeal, pastries, popcorn, white rice, spaghetti.
Alkaline – Potatoes cooked and eaten with the peel.

NUTS

Acid – Cashews, filberts, macadamia, peanuts, pecans, pignolias (pine nuts), pistachios, walnuts, water chestnuts and any nut that is toasted or cooked.
Alkaline – Almonds, brazil, chestnuts.

SEEDS

Acid – Alfalfa, chia, pumpkin, radish, sunflower.
Alkaline – All sprouted seeds, sesame.

OILS

Acid – All animal fats.
Alkaline – Corn, olive.
Neutral – Almond, avocado, butter, coconut, cream, margarine, safflower, sesame, soy, sunflower.

SUGARS

Acid – Brown, cane, malt, maple syrup, milk, molasses, powdered, white.
Alkaline – Honey

MISCELLANEOUS FOODS & BEVERAGES

Acid – Alcoholic beverages, coffee, coffee substitutes, caffeine drinks, drugs, gelatins, maté, nutritional yeast, soy sauce, tobacco, all refined and processed foods.
Alkaline – Agar agar, brewer's yeast, miso, seaweeds.
Alkaline Teas – Alfalfa, clover, mint, sage, strawberry.

DIET FOR TRANSMUTATION AND ASCENSION

Reduce:

Meat
Eggs
Wheat
Dairy Products

Eat no:

Refined, processed, enriched, chemicalized preserved sugars, salts and foods

Why reduce meat? When an animal is slaughtered its flesh records the *feeling* of great fear it experiences. This fear is stamped into its dying flesh through the animal's emotional body. This destructive emotion is then assimilated by the person who eats this flesh. Other hormones, free radicals and inappropriately high amounts of neurotransmitters are absorbed as well. These have a tendency to condense in our brain and affect the thalamus, hypothalamus, pituitary and pineal glands.

An exception to this arises for those cultures that principally eat meat for immediate survival. Some talk to these animals, apologize to them and make amends with them for the taking of life. Mostly this is wild game. The meat of today is highly chemicalized, being fed all sorts of artificial substances to quickly fatten them for the kill. This relates to domestic beef, pork, and chicken.

With the heavier red meats, the body interprets ingestion as cannibalism and thinks it is digesting itself. If you feel the need for meat, however, I suggest baked white fish, no more than three times a week. If red meat is used, sip a glass of concord grape wine during the meal over a thirty minute period. Be sure to kosher red meat to remove poisons.

Why reduce dairy products? Milk, particularly the homogenized, pasteurized, processed type, is highly mucous forming unless it comes straight from mother's breast in the infant years. Pasteurized cheese can also be very mucous forming. Mucous blocks light and retards ASCENSION. If you feel you must have these, use the purest goat's milk and feta cheese possible. Small amounts of pure butter are acceptable as well. Margarine is unacceptable.

Why reduce eggs? Eggs are also mucous forming. If you feel you need eggs, eat only the yolks and no more than five a week. Either ingest these raw, coddled, soft-boiled, or poached.

Why reduce wheat? Gluten forms a glue in the intestine and clogs it. Indeed bread is certainly the staff of life, but not the only staff we need. Why not eat rice, rye, pumpernickel, soy or millet bread? The most highly recommended is essene bread, made of crushed rye sprouts baked at a very low temperature. It is alkaline-forming in nature. Essene bread is definitely the type of staff that could support us and truly lead to life (ASCENSION). Another usable exception to this is sprouted wheat and other grain breads which are now available. Wheat, whether it be whole or not, is mucous forming and acidic if not sprouted. Again, excess mucous equals a blockage of light and reduced light leads eventually to body disruption and death.

I have personally seen numerous cases of allergic responses from people sensitive to wheat. In most cases, this was unknown to them even though they were tested conventionally for allergies.

Refined foods, sugars and salts are *very highly* acidic and mucous forming. Eat these with any regularity at all and you are clearly choosing death.

The ratio of eating 80% alkaline forming foods to 20% acid forming foods is again stressed. It is one point that I highly suggest be followed from the very beginning. As a guide, eat six out of eight of your foods through the day from the alkaline-forming list.

Ease into this diet at a pace you can handle.

CLEANSING

Accumulation of poisons create a state of tissue acidity which afflicts 75% of the world population. Further, this excessive acidity is usually mucous in nature and protein in structure. So there exists a state of trapped mucous acid proteins that inhibit many functions, starting at the cellular level. Ingest pure substances that will help dissolve and eliminate these trapped mucous acid proteins.

I stand on the shoulders of many other giants in the field of corrective nutrition and physiology to bring this to you.

1) Betaine Hydrochloride and Pepsin - There is simply no way to underestimate the vast need for this substance. The deficiencies in people everywhere are pandemic. Hydrochloric acid is very necessary to break down all sorts of proteins so that they feed our cells and sustain us until such time that we can organize and utilize our feelings in such a manner as to express joy continously. Take one tablet 5 minutes before each meal to assist in digestion. If you take hydrochloric acid *do not* take food enzymes at the same time.

2) Other Digestive Enzymes - These may be comfrey, bromelain, papain, and pancreatic enzymes of various types. Some are in combination with Betaine Hydrochloride. These also are very important. Consult your health professional or use your intuition when picking them.

3) Food Enzymes - These are Protease, Amylase, Lipase and Cellulase. This is to be taken with your meals 2-3 times a day and two at night before retiring. Food enzymes help you to digest food as well as dissolve mucous. The extra two at night are specifically recommended for mucous dissolution.

4) Acidophilus - Take 2-3 capsules two times a day and two at night before bed like food enzymes. Acidophilus balances the intestinal tract to allow for better assimilation and elimination of foodstuffs.

5) Liquid Minerals - These come from numerous sources with various brand names, and are similar in their action. They contain multiple minerals in the proper combinations for body usage and elimination of mucous products. It is highly advised that you start very slowly with these as you will find they can have quite an impact upon the system. Generally, if enough ounces are ingested in a day's time, diarrhea will occur. This is the start of excessive mucous being stripped from the walls of the intestines. Further, these minerals rebuild the pancreas and all aspects of the nervous system. They aid in the production of hormones and enzymes. They help the body to quickly rejuvenate.

6) Herbal Bowel Tonics - There are many of these. They come in capsules and powderized herbal formulas. Some of these are to be mixed with water and taken morning and night. Combinations containing Cascara-Sagrada and Senna are the most preferred. Such herbal bowel combinations can be found at health food stores. Recommended dosages will vary. Start with 1 capsule, 2 times a day and do not exceed 3 capsules, 3 times a day without your doctor's supervision. Or, stir one teaspoon 2 times a day in water. Taken carefully, these substances can be quite effective in the elimination of bodily poisons. In liquid or tea form, Swedish Bitters and Super Dieter's Tea are two that are very good.

7) Fletcher's Castoria® for Children - This is a very fine formula and can clean the colon of poisons in a safe and

218

effective manner. It is composed partly of Senna. Start with 2 teaspoons and don't go beyond 4. Take at night before bed.

8) Fo-Ti-Tieng and Gotu Kola - These wonderful herbs are designed to help detoxify the pineal gland. The pineal gland is the principal source of light reception in the body. In most people, it is at least partially calcified and toxic. For ASCENSION to occur this gland must be completely functional. Otherwise crucial hormones will not be produced.

Fo-Ti-Tieng is also a further support and positive stimulus for the adrenal glands which are extremely important for overall health and vitality. Take Fo-Ti-Tieng and Gotu Kola, 2 capsules of each 3 times a day. These herbs heal many aspects of brain function as well.

9) Senna Leaf Tea - The value of this tea must never be underrated. It can be of inestimable service to you. When I asked an ASCENDED ONE about Senna leaf tea he stated simply, "It clears the brain waters." In physiological terminology, the brain waters are cerebro-spinal fluid. It is a transparent fluid, produced in the brain, with a specific ionic nature that bathes both the brain and the spinal column. Through a past buildup of mucous forming protein acid wastes, cerebro-spinal fluid becomes chemically altered and toxic. This impure continuous toxic bath within the central nervous system can lead to calcification of brain tissue, loss of memory, loss of mental acuity, and generalized sluggishness.

Senna is also considered a bowel cleanser. It is recommended that at least one cup be taken each day, unless abdominal cramping occurs.

10) Chlorophyll - The need for chlorophyll in the body is paramount. This may be in a liquid, tablet or powdered form. It is a major alkalizing substance which helps negate the effects of too much mucous formed protein acid trapped in the body. It further aids in the formation of healthy blood and proper pH blood balance. Another powerful health producing quality is that the amount of oxygen is significantly increased by chlorophyll ingestion. This increased oxygenation in the system has many far reaching implications. Some of these are increased blood circulation, better oxygenation to the brain, increased hemoglobin balance and transport of nutrients across the lung membranes. One teaspoon two times a day in water is recommended if a liquid. Other types of chlorophyll dosages vary. It would be very difficult to take too much. The best chlorophyll is fresh liquified greens.

11) Calcium - This element is needed by every cell in the body. For it is the foundation element. Without proper calcium, we decay quickly. Use calcium in conjunction with hydrochloric acid and magnesium for increased absorption. Chew or break these tablets in half, otherwise they do not absorb well. Capsules are preferable. Antacid compounds are not recommended.

12) Bio-Strath® - This formula was derived many years ago in Europe and is an active wild yeast that has digested within itself numerous added wholesome herbs. It is a safe product, and is unquestionably among the most nutritionally valuable products on this planet. It is recommended here as a reasonable way for you to complete your other nutritional needs outside of the specific ones I have outlined. I prefer it because multiple vitamin and mineral suupplements are too varied in their effect upon each individual and should be taken carefully. Bio-Strath®, however, is safe for most situations. (Individuals with yeast allergies are advised to consult their doctor before taking.) This is an excellent formulation for an ASCENDING public. Take at least one teaspoon, two to three times a day.

13) Cayenne Pepper - This dynamic healer is good for so many physical ailments that it would be too lengthy to mention them here. For our purposes it increases endocrine system function and circulation, particularly the adrenal glands. The adrenal glands give fire to the body. Dosages vary between 500 mg. and 5000 mg. a day. In winter, sprinkle a little in your shoes to warm cold feet.

14) Bee Pollen and Propolis - These excellent substances are principally for increased adrenal function and overall endocrine potency. Dosages are variable. Use as much as you like. It is quite unlikely that you would get too much.

15) Skin Brushing - The skin is your largest organ. It is many times the most toxic one I see. Skin brushing helps to loosen the excess wastes on the surface of the skin that regular bathing misses. Skin brush *before* taking a shower or bath. Brush toward the heart in a circular motion starting from any point on the body. Do not brush your face as the bristles are too hard for this. Skin brushing helps promote better colon function as well. Vegetable fiber skin brushes are recommended over natural boar bristle brushes. These can be purchased in most health food stores.

16) Colonic Irrigation - This is a mild procedure that should be done and monitored by a professional in this field. It involves using water to clean the large intestine (colon). As you increase your health by taking the aforementioned acid and mucous removing substances, the colon will many times not be able to move out the increased accumulated wastes fast enough. In this case, a colonic is highly recommended. How often you need one should be up to your therapist, doctor and most importantly, your *feelings*. It has been observed again and again by this writer that if an individual develops even the least symptom of a runny nose, general weakness, fever, any discomfort whatsoever, that these symptoms will greatly reduce and in many cases even vanish after a good colonic irrigation. So many books have been written on the subject of colon health that I am just giving you the rudiments of what is actually happening. From the standpoint of achieving Stage IV and Stage V, Transmutation and ASCENSION, I can say however, that a congested, toxic colon is a definite choice toward death.

I have found another alternative to having a colonic by a therapist is by using a Colema Board®. These were developed by V. E. Irons. It is essentially a home colonic unit. This solves many of the problems of not being able to get a colonic when you need one. The use of the Colema Board®, however, is not exactly the same as a colonic irrigation. The difference is that a colonic is more stimulating and corrective. Further, a colonic stimulates the colon and kidneys for a couple of days after it is given. The Colema Board® is a safe and highly effective method of cleaning yourself whenever you feel the least fatigued, stuffy or under the weather. Remember, if you feel anything less than in great health, colon cleansing is recommended.

Other books by Dr. Baroody:

Hiatal Hernia Syndrome: Insidious Link to Major Illness

The Brotherhood of Intuition

Available from:
Eclectic Press
205 Pigeon St.
Waynesville, NC 28786